THE BEAST IN ME

THE BEAST IN ME

Die to Live

Evelyn A. Johnson

The Beast in Me
Die to Live!

We all are in a daily fight! We have no choice in this matter, we will have to fight. If we must fight, fight to win! We all have a beast living inside of us. We ignore it, we compromise with it, justify it, and feed it, pamper it, dress it up, but it is still there! The beast is waiting and wanting to have its own way!

The beast has been with us all our lives. When we wake up, the beast is there. We go to sleep—my God, the beast is there too! Have you ever wondered why you do the things you do? Why do you think negatively? Why it seems as if I just cannot change? These are some of the questions that you might have that will be answered in this book.

This is a book to help reveal the core of who we are, identify the true enemy that resides within so that we can take authority, and have a victorious life.

Come let us discover and get a closer view of *the Beastly Spirit!*

Die to Live…

Dedication

To my husband, Cleophas, I love you. Thank you for loving me and praying for me. Thank you for allowing me to be me. Thank you for encouraging me to soar! I could not have written this book without you. You are the half that makes me whole. I love you.

To my son, C. Charles, I love you. Thank you for being my prayer partner. Thank you for your excitement and encouraging words of "you got this, Mom" you are my inspiration! Never stop praying and living for God.

To Temple of Prayer Church Family, I love you all. Thank you all for allowing me to serve. Thank you for letting your light shine for Jesus. Thank you for being my family of love. You all are amazing!

To everyone that will read this book, I love you. Thank you for allowing me to be a part of you through this book. May your lives be forever blessed!

Die to Live…

Table of Contents

Foreword

When Evelyn Johnson asked me to write a forward for *The Beast in Me*, I was more than honored. I had the privilege of teaching her wonderful son in high school, and through Charles, I recognized the godly character which so pervades this whole family. Such love for God and His ways is clearly the essence and focal point of this wonderful book.

The apostle Paul tells us in Galatians 5:17 that from birth to death, there is a constant war between the things of the Spirit and the things of the world. Our two natures continually vie for our attention, and the resultant frustrations are our daily struggle.

The Beast in Me beautifully and successfully prescribes—from God's Word—the solution to these frustrations. Ms. Johnson carefully and skillfully weaves the prescriptive cure—dying to self, surrendering to God—and putting others first.

As the author so correctly points out, God knew we would all have to struggle with the beast of a self-first attitude—just as Paul did in Romans 7. But God did not leave us without a remedy, and that cure is surrendering to His Spirit. Not always an easy task, as Ms. Johnson freely admits, but a necessary one. We must first die in order to live.

With expertise, Evelyn includes wonderfully applicable personal stories—illustrations for our soul—never forgetting to remind us of our three enemies in this life—the world, the flesh, and the devil. But neither does she ever allow us to lose sight of the overcoming victory through surrender to the Holy Spirit! In a most inspiring conclusion, she skillfully instructs us regarding the armor of God, the necessity of prayer, and the patience of faith.

I seldom recommend reading the closing chapter of a book first. But in *The Beast in Me*, the wonderful prayer of victory through Christ in the last chapter will inspire you to fully appreciate the pathways to that victory, which comprise the first sixteen chapters. She offers the reader prescriptions that work, for they are prescribed by the Great Physician—highly recommended.

Dr. Jerry L. Parks

Lexington Christian Academy

Author of *God, Please Help Me Pray!*

Purpose

The purpose of this book is to let every reader know that to die is to live and that we can obtain victory over our flesh only through Jesus Christ.

Jesus sent a weapon into this world that will help us defeat everything we will face, and that weapon is the Holy Spirit. The Holy Spirit is always with the believer, the saints of God empowering, equipping, leading, guiding, supporting, aiding, and assisting us in every area of our life to obtain victory and, most of all, helping us to die to live!

Dying to the flesh is to live in Christ.

"For I endorse and delight in the Law of God in my inmost self [with my new nature]" (Romans 7:22, AMPC).

Die to Live...

Preface

It comes a time in our lives that we should get tired of doing the same thing and getting the same results. I do not know about you, but I am so sick of me! Sick of my bad thoughts! Sick of my attitudes! Sick of excuses, bad decisions, being on an emotional rollercoaster, sick, sick, sick of the madness of my flesh, and I can go on! I am just sick of my flesh! Self is an enemy to God and His Spirit. It can be said that we humans are *selfoholics*! There is a fight that we must fight daily! Too often in the wrestling match of life, *self* wins! No more! I have made up in my mind to defeat *me*!

Self I serve notice to you that you have been evicted! Jesus is the new owner of my *soul*!

God has given us the power through Jesus to win!

I must win!

I will win!

I am a winner!

"For to me, to live is Christ [He is my source of joy, my reason to live] and to die is gain [for I will be with Him in eternity]" (Philippians 1:21, AMP).

~ Die to Live…~

Introduction

Dear reader, I asked that you read this book with an open mind. When you read this book, it refers to the flesh or self as a beast, please know that I am not saying you are a beast by any means. I am simply suggesting that when we act out of our spiritual character of God and allow the sinful nature to be in control, that is when we take on the beastly spirit or BS. You will see BS throughout the book, simply meaning Beastly Spirit.

First, I want to say that I am no expert, nor do I have a Doctorate degree. But what I do have is the Holy Spirit that knows everything. With much prayer and fasting, I asked God to lead and guide me and give me the words to write this book. I pray this book will be a blessing to every reader and that it will help change the very essence of who you are.

I am so thankful for my Lord and Savior Jesus Christ that has given me the ability to do all things through Him.

Blessings,

Evelyn A. Johnson

Whom have I in heaven but thee? And there
is nothing upon earth that I desire besides thee.
My flesh and my heart may fail, but God is the
strength of my heart and my portion for ever.

Psalm 73:25-26 (RSV)

~ Die to Live…~

The Beastly Spirit

It happens so regularly that it's predictable. The
moment I decide to do good, sin is there to trip
me up. I truly delight in God's commands, but
it's pretty obvious that not all of me joins in that
delight. Parts of me covertly rebel, and just when
I least expect it, they take charge.

Romans 7:22-23 (MSG)

Can you imagine what life would be like if we lived in
the will of God always? What a remarkable life that would be
living in harmony with God. It is God's will that we live a successful life. Sometimes I wonder what would make us as finite
creatures think that we know more than the Creator. God is
the one who made us who we are. God is the one that knows
our very thoughts before we even can think them. He is the
one who knows our today, tomorrow, and our end. Let us surrender to Him and see what a great difference that would be
living in the perfection of peace and assurance.

"However, it is no longer I who do the deed, but the sin
[principle] which is at home in me and has possession of me"
(Romans 7:17, AMPC).

~ Die to Live...~

19

The Beastly Spirit

Let me introduce the BS—the beastly spirit. Many of us do not look at our self as a beast. We would be so offended if someone called us a beast. The first thing that comes to our mind when we hear the word beast is an animal.

Beast is defined as a contemptible person or something formidably difficult to control or deal with (Merriam Webster).

First, let us recognize that our number one enemy is not Satan, it is *self,* our *flesh! The letter "I" is the most powerful letter in the alphabet! This one little letter has caused the deterioration of civilization.*

Looking at the beast as a contemptible person, we can establish that it means to be not worthy of respect or approval, disgraceful, despicable, and distasteful. What a dreadful meaning. Who would want to be a contemptible person before God? Sometimes I wonder how God must feel when we sin. Do we even think about what we are doing is a sin or not? The flesh is so bold that we know to do what is right and yet do not. The Bible says, "God hates sin." Sin is so deadly that it separates the creation from the Creator. Whenever you talk to some people about sin, the first thing they bring up is grace and mercy. Yes, God is merciful and full of grace, but it does not erase the fact that we had sinned before God. I thought about it; sin is like the smell of a dead animal or a dead person. That smell is unbearable to us as humans so just think what sin smells like in the nozzles of God. When we operate in the flesh, we are not pleasing God. We turn our backs to Him for a moment of pleasure. When will we get to the place that we want to please God first? When we allow our flesh to be in control, the flesh is first, not God. When we live in our flesh which is self, we get self-results. All our great plans and goals and everything we do will not be pleasing to God because we are operating out of His will. God's will must be done.

The Beast Must Die

The *beast* must die! Have you ever felt like saying, "My God, my God, why have I forsaken you and forsaken your Word and forsaken your Holy Spirit!"

I asked myself what in the world is going on with me when I know what the Word of God says, but my flesh, the beast in me, won't allow me to accept or do what the Word is saying because I want my way! There are a plethora of things that come to my mind like check your attitude, watch what you say, don't do this or that, it could be something so small or something big, and I know what the Word of God says about it, and I find myself giving in to the beast!

I want my flesh to die! Are you with me? Do you want your flesh to die? Have you ever talked to someone and they know they are operating in the flesh, they know they are sinning or offending God, and you ask them about it, and they give you the scripture, "We die daily" or "We have to work out our own soul salvation." Well, I thought about it, and one word came to my mind, and that excused. Nothing but an excuse! My question is, "Life, we die daily, then when are we going to die?" When will the old me die off so the new me will be revealed? I know people that have been the same way for years! They said, "I am just that way! They are right their way, not God's way." The bottom line is that we just do not want to give over to the will of God or the leading of the Holy Spirit. We want our way and our will! The scripture says, "[Therefore] Anyone who knows the right thing to do, but does not do it, is sinning [for him it is sin]" (James 4:17, EXB).

I personally had to write this book if for no other reason that the "beast in me" would die. The war is so great inside my soul! I need the blazing fire of the Holy Spirit to incinerate the beast that is within me!

"Unto thee, O Lord, do I lift up my soul" (Psalm 25:1, KJV).

~ Die to Live...~

Bewildered by the Beast

Romans 7:15 (AMP) says, "For I do not understand my own actions…I am baffled and bewildered…"

I don't know about you, but so many times in my life, I would look at myself and say, "Who is this? What did I just do?" Our flesh acts on its own. It is quick to move and make decisions. The flesh never takes a break! We are at constant war with the Spirit of God. I have been in the store, and as simple as shopping, you get to the checkout, and the sales lady asks, "Would you like to put your purchase on one of our store cards?" Then if you say, "I do not have your store card." They quickly say, "You can get a card today and save 20 percent." Without hesitation, the flesh decides to get what it wants. If we took the time to just think about the situation and allow the Holy Spirit to guide us, our outcome would be different.

Now let us look at some more serious situations. Just think, if people would have allowed the Holy Spirit to lead, guide, and direct them, the divorce rate would be lower. People would be working different jobs, living in a different place, be healthier, attending a different church, better off financially, different friends, and the list can go on and on.

Have you ever experienced being in a happy mood, and ten minutes later, you are mad or upset over something as simple as a phone call, a comment, a text, email, something you saw on Facebook, etc.?

Once I had a speaking engagement, and I remember the message was, "Living pass your emotions, the flesh is an emotional eater, it feeds off our emotions." I try not to live in the moment, whether it's good or bad, because things change so fast. One of my prayer requests I ask for daily is for the temperance the sobriety of Jesus. I cannot tell you how many bad decisions I have made off emotions! Off the way, I feel. That is a dangerous place to be in. I can hear the words of my pastor, "Never make a decision when you are too happy or too sad." How true that is.

Another prayer request I ask daily for is the mind of Christ. In reading the Bible, I have never read where Jesus made a bad decision. His outlook was always positive and confident. I know some would say, what about in the Garden of Gethsemane. Really? It is this just like the BS always bringing up that one thing you have done. This is one thing you hear people bringing up about Jesus all the time when He had to make the most important decision that would affect the foundation of the world! The beast of the flesh loves to play the same old record over and over and over! I know Jesus was human, but He knew who He was and where He came from and why He was here on the earth. Let us face it the cup He had to drink was a pool of death! All the sins of the world in one drink!

My God! My God! I thank you! We know how awful we feel after we sin, and Jesus had to taste that! He swallowed our sins! Sins of every human being that would be born on this earth! Oh my God! No matter how many times humans sin and repent, it was in that cup! A cup that was not made from porcelain, silver, or gold, but it was made from *love, grace,* and *mercy.* Truly what manner of love is this: we can hardly take a teaspoon of bitter medicine without spitting it out or frowning our faces, and some people even throw it up! What manner of love is this! I cannot wrap my mind around something so acrimonious! Jesus was not exempt from the battle of the flesh. He had to make the greatest decision that would forever change the foundation of the world, and Jesus answered with these words that defeated flesh, "Nevertheless, not my will, but God's will be done." "And being in agony [deeply distressed and anguished; almost to the point of death], He prayed more intently; and His sweat became like drops of blood, falling down on the ground" (Luke 22:44, AMP).

~ *Die to Live...* ~

Not My Will

When Jesus was in the Garden of Gethsemane, He prayed three times to His Father, but it is not recorded that He said *no*. Each time Jesus said, "Not my will thy will be done." It did not take Jesus days or weeks in the garden; it was only for a few hours. How many times has our Father asked us to do something, and we said no, or our actions said no because we did not do what God asked us to do? It took us days, weeks, months, and sometimes years. The enemy in us our flesh, the BS must be crucified that we will come to a willingness to say yes to God. The purposed that we were created for is molded into the will of God. Once we accept the will of God, the BS has no say on the matter. It is then that we can say as Jesus said, "Nevertheless not my will thy will be done."

What indescribable love this is that Jesus endured all the sins of every human being that will ever enter this world. This love is still here today for anyone, and all a person must do is repent of their sins and accept Jesus as Savior, and they will be forgiven. Eternal life in heaven is now theirs. Praise God.

> Because if you acknowledge *and* confess with your mouth that Jesus is Lord [recognizing His power, authority, and majesty as God], and believe in your heart that God raised Him from the dead, you will be saved.

> Romans 10:9 (AMP)

Thank you, Jesus, for all that you have done for humanity to live.

~ Die to Live...~

Transform Your Lives

> [Therefore] Since Christ suffered while he
> was in his body [flesh], strengthen [arm] your-
> selves with the same way of thinking Christ had
> [intention; attitude; resolve]. [Because] The per-
> son who has suffered in the body [flesh] is fin-
> ished with sin [*or* has broken from the power of
> sin]. Strengthen [Arm] yourselves so that you
> will live here on earth [the rest of the time in the
> flesh] doing what God wants [the will of God],
> not the evil things people want [*or* not pursuing
> your own human desires].

1 Peter 4:1-2 (EXB)

If our lives are going to change, we must die to our flesh. Just as Jesus suffered in the flesh even until death, our fleshly mindset must die as well. The fleshly mindset the BS suffers and is in a crucifying state when we do what is right and pleasing to God. Apostle Peter is telling us that when we suffer in the body that we are done with sin. The flesh does not want to die, so when we deny the flesh, it suffers, or as the verse says, "The flesh has broken from the power of sin." The Ampli-fied translation of this same verse tells us to arm ourselves like warriors. We are at war with ourselves. Peter encourages us to strengthen and arm ourselves in Christ so as long as we live on this earth, we will do what God wants and God's will. But if we do not strengthen ourselves in Christ, the flesh will have its own way of pleasing the world and giving into the human appetites and desires.

Let us live the same way Christ did by thinking intention-al, purposeful, and meaningful.

~ Die to Live…~

The Battle with the Beastly Mind

The law is good, then, and the trouble is not there but with *me* because I am sold into slavery with Sin as my owner. I don't understand myself at all, for I really want to do what is right, but I can't. I do what I don't want to—what I hate. I know perfectly well that what I am doing is wrong, and my bad conscience proves that I agree with these laws I am breaking. But I can't help myself because I'm no longer doing it. It is sin inside me that is stronger than I am that makes me do these evil things. I know I am rotten through and through so far as my old sinful nature is concerned. No matter which way I turn I can't make myself do right. I want to but I can't. When I want to do good, I don't; and when I try not to do wrong, I do it anyway. Now if I am doing what I don't want to, it is plain where the trouble is: sin still has me in its evil grasp. It seems to be a fact of life that when I want to do what is right, I inevitably do what is wrong. I love to do God's will so far as my new nature is concerned; but there is something else deep within me, in my lower nature, that is at war with my mind and wins the fight and makes me a slave to the sin that is still within me. In my mind I want to be God's willing servant, but instead I find myself still enslaved to sin.

Romans 7:14-25 (TLB)

So, you see how it is: my new life tells me to do right, but the old nature that is still inside me loves to sin. Oh, what a terrible predicament I'm in! Who will free me from my slavery to this deadly lower nature? Thank God! It has been done]by Jesus Christ our Lord. He has set me free!

Here we see the beast of the flesh at war against the Spirit of God. Apostle Paul was telling us in Romans 7:25 how thankful he was for being delivered through Jesus Christ, but there was still a war going on inside of him. We, too, have been delivered through Jesus Christ. We must realize, just like Paul, that there is a war going on inside of ourselves daily.

Every day we will have to go into battle with ourselves. The greatest fight will always be within because what is inside of us is what is going to come out. We want Christ to come out, but that is not always the case.

As soon as your day starts, the battle is on. It does not matter what the size of the battle, just get ready to fight! It starts with getting out of bed. Do we pray first or just begin getting dress. Do we take out time to greet everyone in the house or don't speak, do we eat something healthy or junk, do we call in sick or go to work, do we wear something that will represent God or the beast, do we take out time to read at least one verse out of the Bible or just watch the news, will we have a pleasant attitude or a brackish one, will we say goodbye to everyone before leaving the house or just walk out, will we drive the speed limit or speed, will we get to work, school or whatever we have to go and have a godly attitude or a beastly one, will we do everything as unto the Lord or try to do as least as possible, will we witness with our life or try to fit in, will we praise God throughout our day or ignore Him, the fight goes on and on!

> But there is something else deep within me,
> in my lower nature, that is at war with my mind
> and wins the fight and makes me a slave to the
> sin that is still within me. In my mind, I want to
> be God's willing servant, but instead, I find my-
> self still enslaved to sin.

Romans 7:23-25 (TLB)

So you see how it is: my new life tells me to do right, but the old nature that is still inside me loves to sin. Oh, what a terrible predicament I'm in! Who will free me from my slavery to this deadly lower nature? Thank God! It has been done by Jesus Christ, our Lord. He has set me free.

~ Die to Live...~

The Mind Is the Control Tower of the Soul

It Is with Our Mind that We Serve God

Thanks be to God [for my deliverance] through Jesus Christ our Lord! So then, on the one hand I myself with my mind serve the law of God, but on the other, with my flesh [my human nature, my worldliness, my sinful capacity—I serve] the law of sin.

Romans 7:25 (AMP)

I am understanding Romans the seventh chapter more than ever. The beast of this world is a mindset. I have come to understand to a greater degree that it is all about the mind! Everything is attached to the mind. Where the mind goes, our body, our actions, our attitudes, and our mouth, etc., will follow. It is no wonder why there are so many commercials and ads on TV, radio, YouTube, Facebook, and emails, etc., because what we see affects our minds.

Have you ever heard this saying, "If the devil got your mind, he got you?" Excuse me for this inaccurate wording, but that is the saying. The combat with the mind is nonstop. Sometimes even in your sleep, the fight is going on. We must always guard our minds. Once something that someone has said, a thought, or something you have seen gets in your mind, it is hard to get it out! If we would safeguard and shield our minds just like we do material things such as our homes, cars, diamonds, and furs, etc., we would be in much better mental soundness of mind. We are what we have been taught. What we have been told has shaped us to be who we are. If you think about it when we go to other countries the people are different in their languages in the way they cook and what foods, they eat and even the way they dress all because of what they have been taught throughout generations.

> Do not be shaped by [conformed to; pressed into a mold by] this world [age]; instead be changed within [transformed] by a new way of thinking [*or* changing the way you think; the renewing of your mind]. Then you will be able to ·decide [discern; test and approve] what God wants for you [is God's will]; you will know what is good and pleasing to Him and what is perfect.
>
> Romans 12:2 (EXB)

This is a good scripture to help us do God's will. For us not to be pressed or compelled into a mold to become like the world, our minds must be changed. This is one of the hardest things to do. The transformation of our mind is a great fight with the beast of the flesh that only God can help us conquer. The questions can be asked, "Why is the mind so unruly?" and "Why is the mind so strong and robust that it refuses to change!" The mind is like a computer that is constantly being imprinted upon and downloads information from words we hear, say, and from what we see. I believe if we "allow" God to change the way we think, then our entire life would change for the better.

I know I said this prior, but I just cannot get from praying this scripture daily: "Let this mind be in you, which was also in Christ Jesus" (Philippians 2:5, KJV).

What a phenomenal mind this must be having the mind of Christ! Can you imagine thinking and processing life like

Jesus? I can hardly wrap my mind around this or comprehend being able to think about how Jesus always thought! And what is so awesome you can have the mind of Christ no matter what your age is!

What an incredible mind to have a mind *filled* with the *Holy Spirit*! *Oh my God!* I cannot imagine Jesus having negative thoughts, stinking thinking, or making bad decisions, or looking at a situation thinking that it is doom and gloom. Jesus had an outlook and perspective of a conqueror; He knew nothing could defeat Him! What a healthy and remarkable life we, too, could live if we accept the mind of Christ and think how Jesus always thought, in everything, and every situation, how astonishing that would be! Father take over our minds, expand our minds to house the Holy Spirit in Jesus's name!

With the mind of Christ, we can have boundless knowledge and wisdom because Jesus knows everything! Whatever we need to know, just ask Him! Praise God!

Jesus is the greatest example! He was slow to speak. He did not just blurt out anything or just talk just to be talking! He made sense when He spoke. He knew who His enemies were, yet He still respectably responded to them. Jesus was not wishy-washy, one day up, one day down. I hear so many people that say that they are Christian using profanity like it is a noun or verb. I cannot imagine Jesus talking using the s-word, f-word, GD-word, etc.; once again, that is just my personal conviction. I do not want to offend or hurt God any more than I have. I want to love Him more and more! Even more is not enough. I love you, *Jesus,* with every beat of my heart.

~ Die to Live…~

The Mind Is the Control Tower of The Soul

A control tower is a central hub that monitors, manages, and controls decisions and execution. It also has the essential technology, organization, and procedures in place to capture and use transportation data to help make both short- and long-term decisions.

Our mind is our personal little world. It is our control tower. The mind is the central hub of our body and soul. Who is controlling your hub?

The mind monitors and screens what comes into it. The mind watches with assistance from the eyes and imputes data into our thoughts. Then it displays what we have thought, then our thoughts become our words, and words become our actions.

"Death and life are in the power of the tongue, And those who love it *and* indulge it will eat its fruit *and* bear the consequences of their words" (Proverbs 18:21, AMP).

I must admit that I am trying to watch the words that I say. This scripture is saying that we are going to suffer or take on the consequences of what we say. I know people who don't think that this scripture is talking about all words we say, but in reading Proverbs 18:21, it clearly says, "Death and life are in the power of the tongue." It does not say only when you speak on certain things or subjects. We have the choice, just like with everything else, to choose what we say. Are we going to choose to do what the word says or what we think the word should say? The Message translation puts it like this: Proverbs 18:21 (MSG), " Words kill, words give life; they're either poison or fruit—you choose."

Selah…

Words are so powerful we should take them extremely seriously. It was because of words that the decay and fall of mankind took place. Genesis 3:1 (EXB) says, "One day the snake said to the woman, 'Did God really say that you must not eat fruit from any tree in the garden?'" Look how *powerful* words are. The serpent only talked to Eve; the snake didn't threaten to hurt or kill her just used words, and she acted on His words. God had given Adam and Eve instructions on how and what to eat in the garden, Eve knew what God said, but the serpent used his deceptive words to get Eve to disobey God. The serpent told Eve in Genesis 3:4 (EXB), "But the snake said to the woman, 'You will [most certainly] not die.'"

Look how powerful words can be, Eve ate of the fruit and died the most momentous death that a person could die, and that is death to life in God. We can no longer take our words lightly. We must know that words can kill or give life and that they are either poison or fruit, and the choice is ours to make. The tongue is a powerful weapon. Words must be spoken in order for something to happen. It's not because of the sound of the words that you hear, whether they are loud or soft, high pitch or low pitch, sweet tone or nasty tone, but it is how the words penetrate and are accepted by the mind. As soon as words are spoken, they enter and infiltrates the mind. The mind at that time has a choice to make either to receive or reject the words that were just spoken.

We have seen the effects of the poison of words that kill. We read or seen on the news where young and old people have committed suicide just from the words "I hate you," "I don't want you anymore in my life," etc. the person speaking these words didn't have a gun or any kind of weapons just venomous words. Negative words have shaped the minds of so many people that some have died, having never fulfilled their potential in life. We need to think before we speak because once the words come out of our mouths, we cannot pull them back in.

> But I tell you, on the day of judgment people will have to give an accounting for every careless *or* useless word they speak. For by your words [reflecting your spiritual condition] you will be justified *and* acquitted of the guilt of sin; and by your words [rejecting Me] you will be condemned *and* sentenced.

Matthew 12:36-37 (AMP)

The choice is ours to speak words of life that will produce fruit. What will it hurt to speak words of encouragement? It will not take anything from you to speak words of life, but what it will do is add character to you. Hebrews 3:13 (NIV) says, "But encourage one another daily, as long as it is called 'Today,' so that none of you may be hardened by sin's deceitfulness." You mean just encouraging someone could keep them from sinning? Let us put this into practice and see how wonderful the results will be!

Life is all about the positive and the negative. Just like the negative words kill, we can speak the positive words to bring forth life. Speak that you can make it! Speak you can do it! Speak you are more than a conqueror! Speak you are special! Speak you are wonderfully made! Speak you are the apple of God's eye! Speak you can do all things through Christ that gives you the strength! Pray these words out loud: Father, in Jesus's name, help me to watch my words and speak life and not negativity from now own in Jesus's name. Amen!

~ *Die to Live...*~

The Mind Is the Control Tower of the Soul

Who is the supervisor of your mind?

The mind supervises, oversees the what, the when, the how we are going to carry out life. The mind controls the body. The body will not do anything until the mind tells it to. The mind tells the body what to do and what to say, and where to go. The mind tells the body when and what to eat, drink, sleep, get up, go to work, what to wear, what to say and what to do, when to text and what to say in the text, when to check our emails, Facebook, Twitter, etc. The mind controls *everything* we do. Our mouth will not speak anything without being filtered through the mind. Our feet will not start walking on their own, the mind must tell them where to go.

The mind knows it is the supervisor of you. We hear people talking about their supervisor at work. They say if they think the supervisor is good or bad, fair or unfair, mean or nice, hot-headed or mild-tempered. Well, just like employees talk about their supervisors, they talk about us as well. What are people saying about the supervisor, our mind? Can they say it is good and not bad, fair or unfair, mean or nice, hot-headed or mild-tempered?

We must conduct (M & M) mind maintenance throughout the day. We must be conscientious of what we are thinking. Wrongful thoughts can creep into our minds, and we do not even notice it because we were distracted. If we do not terminate the wrongful thought, it will linger and grow into trouble, and trouble turns into a battle, and then the fight is on! All of this could have been alleviated if we had protected our minds from the start.

Let's look at some synonyms: adjective of the word negative—adversarial, adversary, antagonistic, antipathetic, hostile, inhospitable, inimical, jaundiced, mortal, unfriendly, un-sympathetic.

Just reading these words, the first thought that came to my mind is the devil! He fits all these words! All these words describe him. You can find the beast of the flesh being demonstrating in these words as well. We are living in a world where we see unfriendly and unsympathetic, hostile, and adversarial people. This is a mean and cruel world we live in! We are experiencing the coldness of the heart and uncaring, insensitive people not only in the world but in the church too! The church has changed drastically. It used to be a time when visitors came to church, and the preached word convicted their heart the visitors would come to the front of the church and give their lives to Christ. If there was anyone in need of prayer, time was taken out for them. Now you can hardly find churches that have an altar call, much less the congregation waiting and being sensitive enough to wait until the hurting, broken, sick, distraught, and suicidal soul and or for soul salvation to take place, or whatever the person was facing for the congregation to wait and pray. The world's system has filtrated itself into the church! In the world, it is all about me, it's doggie dog, ruthless and self-serving, competitive, aggressive, and cheap! Now the world sees the church as cheap!

The beast is in total control! Has the church cheated God right out of His kingdom? Some people have time for everything but God. I once was told after I invited someone to church that they said, "I don't have time for God" I was speechless. One lady told me after she works all week and runs all day on Saturdays for her children that are involved in sports, dance, gymnastics, etc., she keeps Sundays as her rest day because she doesn't want to be tired for her job on Monday. I have also talked to people who say they are Christians but do not have time for God, church, prayer, or reading the

Word. The reason they gave me was they were just too busy. This is one area I believe the devil fights us in, and that is *time*. He knows we cannot redeem the time. He knows if we fill our time up with the things of the world that we will not have space for God. I totally get it about time, and every church must operate the way that fits them. I am a timely person, and I respect the office of time, but there is a time and place for everything. Why is it that we can work eight hours a day, forty hours a week, and only want to give God one an hour or heaven forbid if it is two on Sundays!

The BS loves this so much because the beastly spirit does not want to die! The BS wants as little as possible of God, it wants just enough to say I went to church today. The BS loves the one-way street. One way in, and one way out. I go to church one way and come out the same. How is it that Christians can sit and watch a movie that is two to three hours long and does not want to be disturbed? Some people have told me they will suffer from holding themselves from going to the restroom because they do not want to miss any of the movies! But in the church, you see people up and down and back and forward to the restroom, on their phones, passing notes, talking, sleeping, eating, drinking, and blowing bubbles! God help us! God is the one that gave us the ability to do whatever is that we do. He has given us the ability to walk and talk and use our brains. Everything comes from God, all the gifts and talents come from God. We cannot do anything without God. We cannot even breathe unless God says so! Then we come to church and have the audacity to put God on the clock! *Wow!* Double *wow!*

One day I was trying to watch a basketball game with my husband, and that game went on and on! It went so long I got up and left because they went into overtime! But one thing I noticed that no one left! They all sat right there and cheered their team on. The arena is filled with Christians and non-Christians, and they are all there cheering for their team! What would it look like if the Christians would cheer for Jesus like that? Not worrying about if the praise goes into overtime!

I thought the word Christian meant to be Christ-like. When did Jesus ever put anything before His Father, before the Will of His Father and the purpose He came to earth for? The BS, the beast of the flesh, *self* is winning the fight of life for so many people. If I can get one point over in this book is that we must *die to live!*

Galatians 5:17 tells us that these two forces within us are constantly fighting each other to win control over us! Which one is going to win? The devil wants to win! He will do anything to win! The devil does not fight fair!

The devil is having a field day with people that say they are Christians but live like heathens. The devil wants to win! The devil wants control over us! The devil hates us because God loves us so much!

> For God so [greatly] loved *and* dearly prized the world, that He [even] gave His [One and] only begotten Son so that whoever believes *and* trusts in Him [as Savior] shall not perish, but have eternal life. For God did not send the Son into the world to judge *and* condemn the world [that is, to initiate the final judgment of the world], but that the world might be saved through Him.

> John 3:16-17 (AMP)

The devil does not care how people go to church or how many times a week they go, just as long as they do not live according to the Word of God. The devil wants people to say they are Christians (sheep) but living and dressed in wolves' clothing (heathens). The word heathen sounds strong, but it is in the Bible. The definition of heathen is of or relating to people or nations that do not acknowledge the God of the Bible. The word acknowledge stands out for me. If a person says they are a Christian and do not acknowledge God as accepting His will and His way, living the way the Bibles says, " Recognizing God in their everyday life but ignoring Him by not serving Him in any way of their life." Can it be that they are living in Heathenville?

The BS is a part of the world. The BS opposes God's will and God's way. We must die that Christ lives. Anyone willing to live for Christ can move out of Heathen-Ville at any time. Jesus's altar is always open. You can commune with Him as long as you want. He doesn't wear a watch.

Let us pray that the Holy Spirit will be the supervisor over our mind that we please God in our everyday lives.

> For we naturally love to do evil things that are just the opposite from the things that the Holy Spirit tells us to do; and the good things we want to do when the Spirit has his way with us are just the opposite of our natural desires. These two forces within us are constantly fighting each other to win control over us, and our wishes are never free from their pressures.
>
> Galatians 5:17 (TLB)

~ Die to Live... ~

The Negative Mind

I see why we must have the mind of Christ! The mind of Christ Jesus is positive, versus the mind of the devil is negative. When we have a negative mind, we are thinking like the devil. I believe Jesus was *never negative*! I never read in the Bible where Jesus talked negatively or said negative things.

One thing that will help us to have a positive mind like Jesus is to ask God to give us a sound mind.

Since the mind is our control tower, it certainly must be sound and rational.

Would you want to have someone in the control tower at the airport with an irrational mind? A mind that is illogical and absurd cannot make good decisions. The saying "We are in the situations because of the choices we make" is true. I cannot count how many times throughout my life that I have made bad decisions or made the wrong choice.

Look what the Word is telling us:

> The end *and* culmination of all things is near. Therefore, be sound-minded and self-controlled for the purpose of prayer [staying balanced and focused on the things of God so that your communication will be clear, reasonable, specific and pleasing to Him.]

1 Peter 4:7 (AMP)

Second Timothy 1:7 (AMP) says:

> For God did not give us a spirit of timidity *or* cowardice *or* fear, but [He has given us

a spirit] of power and of love and of sound
judgment *and* personal discipline [abilities
that result in a calm, well-balanced mind and
self-control].

2 Timothy 1:7 (AMP)

~ *Die to Live...* ~

Your Words Frame Your World

Too many times, we allow people's words to frame our world.

Can a person take your mind? I believe they cannot. No one can take your mind; you have to give it to them. God created human beings with one mind, one brain. If a person has more than one brain, they are considered deformed. We must always guard our minds. If you are easy to be persuaded, ask God to give you a strong mind that you will not be so easy to allow what negative people would say causing you to change. If you were on the up having a positive day stay up. Do not let anyone bring you down! Do not let anyone spray you with the raid of negativity. Have you ever noticed that negative people hang out with negative people? It is so funny when a positive person comes around and starts talking positively, the negative people quickly try to shut that person up, or they leave because they like being in the room of negativity! Or the positive person keeps trying to interject positive words, and since the negative Nate will not allow positive patty to change the conversation, then positive patty gets up and leave because they have had enough.

I will never forget a message our pastor preached, and his title was "Your words frame your world." Right here, I want to give a shout-out to all the pastors that are preaching the truth! I want you all to know that we are listening! What you say matters because our lives have been enhanced and changed for the better from the words that you preach and teach. Be encouraged because you are a difference maker!

~ Die to Live…~

The Beastly Mind Is an Enemy to God

For those who are living according to the
flesh set their minds on the things of the flesh
[which gratify the body], but those who are living
according to the Spirit, [set their minds on] the
things of the Spirit [His will and purpose]. Now
the mind of the flesh is death [both now and forever—because it pursues sin]; but the mind of
the Spirit is life and peace [the spiritual well-be-
ing that comes from walking with God—both
now and forever]; the mind of the flesh [with its
sinful pursuits] is actively hostile to God. It does
not submit itself to God's law, since it cannot,
and those who are in the flesh [living a life that
caters to sinful appetites and impulses] cannot
please God. However, you are not [living] in the
flesh [controlled by the sinful nature] but in the
Spirit, if in fact the Spirit of God lives in you
[directing and guiding you]. But if anyone does
not have the Spirit of Christ, he does not belong
to Him [and is not a child of God].

Romans 8:5-9 (AMP)

In writing this book, I cannot express enough how much
we need the Holy Spirit. We cannot have enough of the Spirit
of God. In chapter eight, we see the beast in action. The beastly
spirit mindset is the sinful flesh nature. The Word tells us that
if we follow our sinful or beastly spirit, our minds will want
sinful things, not godly things. If we are thinking and processing with a sinful mind, then the devil can lead and guide us,
and the outcome is never good with our enemy. Let us take

note of some keywords the scriptures are telling us. Verse five points out those who live, follow, think, set on, outlook and shaped by the sinful nature of our flesh the BS only wants what they want not what God wants or what pleases God.

Now let us read what verse six says: "If people's thinking is controlled by [*or* outlook/mind is set on] the sinful self [sinful nature; flesh], there is [the result is] death."

This is serious! If we allow the BS, our sinful mind, to control our thinking our mindset, then the results will be death. Death to what? Death to life! The beastly sinful nature mind produces sin, and nothing dead can bring forth life. The sinful mind is what tells us we cannot, you will not, your nothing, we cannot do what God has given us to do, etc. The sinful mind looks at life through dirty glasses! Whereas the godly mind sees victory, and the BS sinful mind sees doom and gloom. The sinful BS mind is full of negativity, hate, evil, wickedness, lying, prejudice and the list goes on. The BS sinful mind is the devil's playground, and he has so many people on it going around and around on the merry-go-round of death!

"But if their thinking is controlled by [*or* outlook/mind is set on] the Spirit, there is [the result is] life and peace" (Romans 8:6, EXB).

Thank you, Jesus, for the Holy Spirit that brings life and peace to our minds!

Control—define: to have power over *rule*.

The word control is what stands out to me. The verse says our thinking must be controlled by the Holy Spirit. We must give the Holy Spirit power and authority over our thinking, and then we will have life and peace. Isn't that wonderful? Our minds, our thinking needs peace in this perverse world that we are living in. It is so easy for our minds to wander off into *no-no* land when we see what is going on around us, what's on the news, and all the sadness that is spread across the land.

Verse seven is a prime example of why we need the Holy Spirit to control our minds:

> When people's thinking is controlled by [or outlook/mind is set on] the sinful self [sinful nature; flesh], they are against [hostile to] God, because they refuse to obey [submit to] God's law and really are not even able to obey [submit to] God's law
>
> Romans 8:7 (EXB)

"Those people who are ruled by [or under the control of; in] their sinful selves [their sinful nature; the flesh] cannot please God" (Romans 8:7, MSG).

The Bible is amazing! I can see clearly why the sinful BS mind is antagonistic and hostile to God. The sinful nature, BS mind oppose God and the things of God. The definition of mindset is the established set of attitudes held by someone. If a person has an attitude of arrogance to disobey God, then certainly that person can not please God in any way. The Bible says they refuse to obey and submit to God they cannot! The sinful nature mind is the total opposite of the godly nature of the godly mind. In God, there is no sin. We see the sinful beastly spirit mind at work like never before in the history of our nation. There is no need to wonder why people are doing such hideous, dreadful, shocking, repulsive, and gruesome things! The BS is working overtime doing whatsoever it wants, whatever it wills, because of the controlling of the sinful nature that is within.

If we want to please God in every area of our lives, let us give over to the Holy Spirit and let Him control our mind.

~ Die to Live... ~

Mind over Matter

Merriam Webster defines mind over matter used to describe a situation in which someone is able to control a physical condition, problem, etc., by using the mind.

The definition of willpower is energetic determination, control of one's impulses and actions; self-control, restraint, self-command, self-containment, self-control, self-discipline.

It blows my mind when I see people on TV walk on fire! Or do the extremes with their bodies. In the diet world, we are hearing so much about intermittent fasting. For Christians, this is not anything new, but what has captured my mind is that the person that is on a diet because their mind, their will power to lose weight they fast and get results! Some diets now include intermittent fasting for so many hours and so many days, and people are doing it without the help of the Holy Spirit. They have purposed in their mind that they want to lose weight just that bad that they will not eat food. The *mind*! Now, if they can do it with just their willpower, then surely, we can with the help of God.

Once again, looking at willpower, it is defined as control of one's impulses and actions; self-control (control or restraint of oneself or one's actions, feelings, etc.).

> I can do all things [which He has called me to do] through Him who strengthens *and* empowers me [to fulfill His purpose—I am self-sufficient in Christ's sufficiency; I am ready for anything and equal to anything through Him who infuses me with inner strength and confident peace.]

Philippians 4:13 (AMP)

Do we really believe this? In reading this verse from the Amplified, what stands out is that we can do all things that God has called us to do, not all things that I want to do, here we see again God's will. If we do His will, God will strengthen and empower us to fulfill His purpose that He created us to do on this earth.

It is all about two words, will and power!

God's will and His power! ~

For the beast to die, we must have willpower, determination, and fortitude to do God's will, and most certainly, we need to be filled with His Power, the Holy Spirit.

~ Die to Live... ~

The Power of the Beast

It Is When Self Dies, Christ Is Made Alive

One of the definitions of power is the capacity or ability to direct or influence the behavior of others or the course of events. Synonyms: influence, authority, sway, control, say, ascendancy, dominance, advantage, pressure.

The beastly spirit is formidably difficult to control or to deal with. The beastly spirit is immensely powerful and strong. Look at Satan's known beast. He is powerful and strong. He can direct, supervise, and influence a person that is powerless or does not have the power of God. The devil can sway, control, and pressure a person to do things they never thought in their life they would do!

Let us not fool ourselves. The devil is stronger than we will ever be in the flesh. That is why it is imperative that we have the Holy Spirit! One thing for certain is that the devil can n*ever defeat* the *God* that has *all* power and reign supreme! The God of the Bible! The God of Abraham, Isaac, and Jacob! He is our God, the true and living God Jehovah is His Name!

The power of the flesh of the beast is so powerful that it fights against the very purpose God created us for! This unbearable beast of flesh fights against God! This flesh, the BS, has the audacity to fight against the Holy Spirit and the will of God! The flesh is even more powerful than a hurricane or a tornado! These horrific storms come and cause damage for a short period of time, but the flesh can cause continuous damage, even death to the soul!

~ Die to Live…~

The Crucified Flesh

I believe that if self, the BS, was crucified, we would love God and the things of God even more. Loving people would not be an issue because God is love. We would strive to live the word out and study it more. Our prayer life would be enhanced to the maximum!

Prayer

Prayer is an area that I know about personally. There is a reason why the Bible says to pray without ceasing! Whenever you purpose in your mind to pray, the flesh will tell you, "You are tired, do it tomorrow my pastor is praying for me," or this is the big one "Jesus is sitting at the right hand of the Father making intercession praying for me right now!" The flesh is selfish and sinful and does not want to give into righteousness. I have been taught this saying, "Little prayer, little power. Much prayer, much power!" and how true that is. The devil does not want us to be powerful! Just think, if the beast of flesh, self, was crucified, we would fulfill the purposes in our lives. We would accomplish the nevertheless not my will, but God's will be done. I believe if the beast of the flesh, the BS was dead, the church would be effective in every area of kingdom work because we would be operating in the Holy Spirit. No more pew warmers! Everyone would be working in their callings and purposes. We would be honest in tithing and offering. The praise and worship would be amazing! There would be a oneness that would unify every heart, mind, and soul in the place, and as a result, great signs of the miraculous would be prevalent in the churches! Healthy thinking, no more stinking thinking, fault finding, murmuring, or complaining. More importantly, when people visit the church, they would be welcomed and loved without dissimulation. How marvelous that would be!

The Beastly Spirit ~ Gratification

Gratification—pleasure, especially when gained from the satisfaction of a desire.

Synonyms: satisfaction, fulfillment, indulgence, appeasement, assuagement, pleasure, enjoyment.

The beast wants its way. Another fortress of power we can contribute to the BS is egotistical self-gratification. It is so obvious to the spiritual eye to see people out of order in the kingdom. It is time for the church to get back in order, get back into its rightful place, and with God's help, we can do it. I always wonder why the laity thought that it was their job to tell the pastor what to do. I have never seen or read where the sheep begin to talk and tell the shepherd what to do. Can you imagine the sheep telling the shepherd, "Don't feed me green grass, or why can't I run wild and get out of this gate?" Even if a church has a committee board, the final answer is made by the leader, or it should be.

Now the LORD said to Moses, "Come up to Me on the mountain and stay there, and I will give you the stone tablets with the law and the commandments which I have written for their instruction." So, Moses arose with Joshua his attendant, and he went up to the mountain of God. And he said to the elders, "Wait here for us until we come back to you. Remember that Aaron and Hur are with you; whoever has a legal matter, let Him go to them." Then Moses went up to the mountain, and the cloud covered the mountain.

Exodus 24:12-15 (AMP)

There are many examples in the Bible of God talking to one person. I thought about when God wanted to talk to Moses or give him instructions. God did not call for the people, nor did God ask for the leaders to accompany Moses. Unfortunately, when more than one person is being given information, sometimes it is repeated differently. You can have a group of people watching the same news being reported about an accident, and each one will have a different view from what they have seen. God has set up an order for a reason. God knew the beast the flesh would want to have its way. We can be sure of this where there is no order chaos is in the midst!

~ Die to Live...~

The Beastly Spirit—Crucifixion

How phenomenal it would be if the crucifixion of the beast of the flesh was pervasive in preachers, teachers, evangelists, or anyone who teaches the Word, etc., the Word of God would go forth in the authority of the Holy Spirit. There would be a greater anointing attached to the word, which would cause yokes to be destroyed and souls saved, delivered, and set free. When the beast of the flesh is crucified, preachers of the gospel would get their messages straight from the throne of God, not relying on themselves or the internet or listening to someone else's messages and repeating it. The Rhema Word of God would flow straight from the throne because the Holy Spirit would feed it to the mind. When we operate out of the will of God, self is the only one being gratified, *not* God. If we want the anointing to be with us, then self the BS must die that Christ lives. Luke 22:42 (KJV) says, "Saying, Father, if thou be willing, remove this cup from me: nevertheless not my will, but thine, be done."

~ Father, help us to be attentive to your voice and surrender to your will in Jesus name ~

~ Die to Live…~

Evelyn A. Johnson

The Battle with the Gluttony Beast

I could write a whole new book on the subject of weight loss!

> I can anticipate the response that is coming: "I know that all God's commands are spiritual, but I'm not. Isn't this also your experience?" Yes. I'm full of myself—after all, I've spent a long time in sin's prison. What I don't understand about myself is that I decide one way, but then I act another, doing things I absolutely despise. So, if I can't be trusted to figure out what is best for myself and then do it, it becomes obvious that God's command is necessary.

> Romans 7:15-16 (MSG)

Wow, this translation is to the point! The BS, beastly spirit is so full of itself! One of the biggest fights for a lot of human beings is food. The beast is very smart! It knows if you nibble a little and keep nibbling soon, the whole cake will be gone! That is how sin is. The devil gets us to nibble and nibble a little, then *oops*, we find ourselves back in the sin prison, being eaten up with guilt and shame!

The torture of culpability, disgrace, and embarrassment has caused so many to quit on life and even God. Don't quit, and don't give up. This is a conspiracy of the devil to get people to give up on everything and especially on God, whatever you do not give up! Do not quit! Grab on cling to Jesus like never before, and He will help you through whatever you are facing rather is self-control with eating or whatever is binding you.

We serve a great God that no matter what we have done, no matter what sins we have committed, God is just and will forgive us.

~ Die to Live... ~

The Food Fight!

I need God in every area of my life, and weight loss is one of them. I know I am not alone in this battle. Statistics show that an estimated one hundred sixty million Americans are either obese or overweight, and that was in 2014! I have been on the rollercoaster of weight loss for years! I know I need to lose weight for various reasons, and I still allow the fight with the BS to win. Being overweight is not healthy. It causes so many health problems, and yet still, when pizza, cookies, cake, and ice cream, etc., is placed in front of me, the will of me, the BS takes control! I say, "How can I have the Holy Spirit the power of God living inside of me and don't have enough power to say no to food?" The power is there, but it is called "override!" We can overrule the Holy Spirit at any time, which is not good for us to do. Even though food is one of the flesh's chief areas, we have the power to say no through the Holy Spirit. All we must do is stop ignoring the Holy Spirit to satisfy the flesh. The results of disobedience to the Holy Spirit are always a debauched outcome! If we think about it, it is a temporary fulfillment. Once the cookies, cake, pizza, ribs, chicken, or whatever your favorite food is are gone, it is gone! The taste is gone, the food is gone, and all we have left to show is extra! Extra weight! Feeling stuffed and miserable! All the fighting and wrestling we do in our minds, should I eat it or not, we do it all for a taste that will only last while it is in your mouth. *Omg*! Help us, Lord!

I often wonder why it is that when I am on a consecration that I can fast without food for days. I am talking twenty-one days, seven days, three days, and I have even gone forty days on the Daniel fast, but when it comes to just simply eating right, it's a struggle. The flesh is something to reckon with! The BS does not want to die! I had to remind myself:

I can do all things [which He has called me to do] through Him who strengthens *and* empowers me [to fulfill His purpose—I am self-sufficient in Christ's sufficiency; I am ready for anything and equal to anything through Him who infuses me with inner strength and confident peace.]

Philippians 4:13 (AMP)

Be encouraged we can defeat the beast even when it comes to food! We got this! Thank you, Holy Spirit!

~ Die to Live ~

Fasting Will Kill the Flesh

I absolutely love it when I am fasting. My heart, mind, and soul are totally on God. I am trusting, believing, praising, and reading God's Word. Every beat of my heart is saying, "Lord, I love You, Lord I need You." When I am fasting, everything in life looks different. I see things differently, hear with clarity. There is calmness and peace inside of my soul that cannot be explained. It is no wonder why the enemy fights against us when we fast. Why would he want us to have peace of mind and a settle-ness that calms the red seas in our lives? The devil does not want us to pray and certainly not too fast.

When we abstain and reframe from food, I can perceive spiritually as if my body is being stripped away layer by layer from the things of the flesh. The BS is strong-willed, and it takes a stronger power than us to defeat it. When we fast, we are putting our flesh on shut down and giving over to the power of the Holy Spirit. I believe if we can conquer the food rapacious spirit, then we can control anything in our lives!

When we fast, we are shutting down the rubbish of the flesh. If we want our attitudes tamed and under control, then fast, if we want self-control over our mouth rather is from food, saying harmful and negative words, or just talking too much, fast. If we are dealing with a situation that we cannot figure out the answer to or we need to make a serious decision, fast. If we feel ourselves drifting away from God, prayer, reading the Word, fast. Fasting breaks the chains of things that have us bound as well as putting things together all at the same time.

The Bible is clear on the results from fasting. Fasting helps to crucify the beast in us. This is war! Remember, the war is between the beast and the Holy Spirit. We must use something stronger than ourselves. Fasting empties out self and gives space for the Holy Spirit to dwell. The anointing of God is poured out even more when we fast. The Bible lets us know that it is with the anointing that yokes are destroyed. When fasting, we become closer to God. Everything is shut *out* as we shut *in* with *God*. What an exceptional time it is when it is no longer I but Christ that live.

~ Die to Live…~

Lights out—Blackout

God Is Light

This is the message [of God's promised revelation] which we have heard from Him and now announce to you, that God is Light [He is holy, His message is truthful, He is perfect in righteousness], and in Him there is no darkness at all [no sin, no wickedness, no imperfection]. If we say that we have fellowship with Him and yet walk in the darkness [of sin], we lie and do not practice the truth; but if we [really] walk in the Light [that is, live each and every day in conformity with the precepts of God], as He Himself is in the Light, we have [true, unbroken] fellowship with one another [He with us, and we with Him], and the blood of Jesus His Son cleanses us from all sin [by erasing the stain of sin, keeping us cleansed from sin in all its forms and manifestations]. If we say we have no sin [refusing to admit that we are sinners], we delude ourselves and the truth is not in us. [His word does not live in our hearts.] If we [freely] admit that we have sinned *and* confess our sins, He is faithful and just [true to His own nature and promises], and will forgive our sins and cleanse us *continually* from all unrighteousness [our wrongdoing, everything not in conformity with His will and purpose]. If we say that we have not sinned [refusing to admit acts of sin], we make Him [out to be] a liar [by contradicting Him] and His word is not in us.

1 John 1:5-10 (AMP)

~ Die to Live... ~

The Beast Come Out at Night

Have you ever thought about why it is when you are in a dark place in your heart and mind that is when the attacks from the enemy are the greatest?

The word dark means with little or no light. It is no wonder why the devil torments and plagues our minds in the dark. Our minds cannot see! When our minds are in the dark, it is clouded with gunk, doom, and gloom! We cannot think or process life properly if our minds are dark. Nor can we handle what we are facing appropriately if our minds are being bombarded with hopelessness and despair.

Imagine being in a physical storm at noon driving home. It appears to be night because of the dark clouds covering the sun. Trying to drive in the dark in a storm is difficult. It takes a strong positive mind to press through the darkness in a storm. I have seen cars pulled over to the side of the road because they cannot see. This is what has happened to some people when they are in a dark situation. They have pulled off to the side of the road of life and stop driving towards God. Darkness is a scare tactic for some people. Even some adults still must sleep with the lights on.

Darkness can spread and bring fear because you cannot see. We should not be afraid of the dark because the darkness has no power! It produces no power! Can you grab darkness? Darkness is like the wind—you cannot grab it. Think about this: the only way darkness has power is that we must give power to it. If you are in a room and the lights are off, the room is dark. The only way darkness will leave is that we must physically get up and turn the lights on; we must get up and give it power by turning on the switch. Let us not give the enemy any power. Keep your lights on. We all have an electric bill, and if we do not pay our bills, the electric company will turn your power off. They do not care if you have children or the elderly in your home; they will shut your power off for non-payment. This is what the devil is trying to do. He is trying to shut your power off! Make sure the bill has been paid! With God, you have unlimited power! Jesus paid our bill on the cross, now all we have to do is stay plugin by praying, fasting, reading the Word, praising and worshipping God, and assembling ourselves with another believer. Stay connected!

~ Die to Live...~

Jesus Is the Light, Power, and Our Source!

The *Son* brings power! Jesus is the power source! Jesus is the light of the world! Father, make us a bigger light! We want to be so powerful and bright that whatever situation we are facing or wherever we go, we want to bring light into the situation that would cause it to switch the outcome to a victorious one!

Have you ever experienced your lights going off in your home when it is storming? What an uncomfortable feeling. I hate it because I cannot see! I bump into things that have been there for years. I have gotten hurt because I could not see what was in front of me. Spiritually we can get hurt as well. Our decisions get clouded and dark, and we make the wrong choice. We run into situations and cannot seem to get out of the maze of mess! It is only when the light comes, we can see! Jesus is the light. He can bring clarity to any situation, brighten up any room in your heart, and shine directly on what we might have thought was lost. Jesus is the light of the world! Praise Him!

~ Die to Live...~

The Eye Is the Lamp of Your Body

The eye is the lamp of your body. When your eye is clear [spiritually perceptive, focused on God], your whole body also is full of light [benefiting from God's precepts]. But when it is bad [spiritually blind], your body also is full of darkness [devoid of God's word].

Luke 11:34 (AMP)

How interesting is this scripture from Luke 11:34, "The eye is the lamp to our body"? How fascinating to picture this! Imagine lamps where your eyes are located. If the lamp is off, it's dark, and you cannot see. The Word says that when our eye is clear, we have spiritually perceptive, or we are sensitive, observant, and discerning with an understanding of God's instructions, His principals, rules, and God's teaching. But when it is bad spiritually blind, your body also is full of darkness devoid of God's Word. That means the lamps, our eyes are off! We are spiritually blind, and our bodies are full of darkness! *Oh*, my goodness! Full of darkness and bereft and empty from God's Word! It is no wonder why the devil wants us to stay in the dark! He does not want us to know the truth, the word which brings forth light, life, and liberty!

I pose a question spiritually "How can we see if we are in a dark place?"

You can tell, "If a person is blind by the way they move their bodies." Their bodies are not limber or actively moving because they cannot see. They move slowly, feeling their way, or someone has to lead them. I am only using this as an analogy; please do not think I am saying anything bad about blind people, I am just trying to make a point. Not one blind person probably if you asked them, "Do you want to be blind or would you rather see?" they would most likely say they want to see. Spiritually we should want to see it as well. Let us stay focus and connected to God so that our lights will never go out.

~ Die to Live...~

When Darkness Takes Over Your Mind

This is a personal experience I went through with my husband, who is my pastor. We were in the process of purchasing the church that we were in for over eight years. A former leader in our organization gave his word that he could help us to get the money to purchase the church. This process was going on for months.

My husband was truly clear from the beginning with the leader that if he could not do this, please let him know so that he could go to our bank to acquire the loan. The leader said, "Son, you don't have to do that. I can take care of this for you." Week after week, we were told the money is coming. My husband was told that the money is going to be wired on a certain day, that did not happen. In the meantime, our leader was in contact with the sellers at the other church. He assured them that everything was being worked out, and they had his word.

During this time, our pastor was letting the leadership and the church know what was going on. Our hopes were high! We had begun to plan our victory celebration service!

The day came, and we were given a closing date to meet with the other church.

Everybody was there. Their board and their lawyer and my husband and myself. The phone rang, and our leader began to talk with such persuasiveness about the process of retaining the money. Have you ever heard of the gift of gab? Well, he has it! I told my husband that our leader could sell someone a flat tire, and they would buy it. As we were sitting at the closing meeting, everything was going well until suddenly, in the middle of the conversation, our leader said, "Something has happened to the money! Let me see why the money hasn't been transferred to your bank. *Oh* no, my heart sunk! Here we go again!" He took us around and around. After a couple of hours, we ended the meeting. How disappointing and humiliating. This buying process had gone on for months and now has taken its toll on everyone involved. But that was not the end of it. Our leader asked them to give him until the end of the week, they agreed. The end of the week came with another excuse!

I must say the other church showed the love of Christ during the whole ordeal. There were never any harsh words or attitudes expressed. Only love and kindness were given to us at the highest degree. We could tell they were trying everything they could on their end to make this happened.

In this process, we lost over two million dollars dealing with our leader because we had to sell our land trying to hold on to the church as well as all the thousands we had given, the members, our families, and friends.

As time went on, my husband begins to get so frustrated and upset because he could not believe our leader, who called him his son, would lie to him and cause us to lose our church. Depression and unhappiness set in his heart, and this would be the start of a journey of fighting the faith that he would experience.

This was when the darkness came over my husband. My husband's countenance changed. I am referring to the spiritual change on his face. I could see it if no one else could see the sadness, shame, disgust, disappointment, and madness in every frown and every sorrowful tear that fell from his eyes.

I remember walking in his office at the church, seeing him mystified holding a towel as the rivers of pain ached from his heart as he sat there playing the song "You're My Only Help" by Tye Tribbit…

I quietly walked out of his office and closed the door, and said a tender prayer. He had a few minutes to gather himself before he went into the sanctuary. No matter what he was experiencing, I knew he would stand in the strength of God as he walked out of his office to go and give the morning message to a congregation that had no clue of the ripped and torn man that stood before them. Only God can take us through a hurt that wounds the soul.

I must say I cannot remember what the message was about, but I do know He gave it His all! He told us He did not know but one speed and that is 100 percent when doing things for God—the church is a witness—even to this day, our Pastor always gives 100 percent of what He has.

~ Die to Live...~

The Holy Spirit Reveals What Is in the Dark

> And [I pray] that the eyes of your heart [the
> very center and core of your being] may be en-
> lightened [flooded with light by the Holy Spirit],
> so that you will know *and* cherish the hope [the
> divine guarantee, the confident expectation] to
> which He has called you, the riches of His glori-
> ous inheritance in the saints (God's people).

Ephesians 1:18 (AMP)

I began praying and fasting. I sought God for direction. I prayed, asking God for the Holy Spirit to lead and guide my husband and for God's will to be revealed. I know for a fact that when you call on Jesus, you are calling the light into your situation. Only the light of Christ could shine through the darkness of hurt and pain my husband was suffering.

As time went on, not only I could see the hurt and pain he was feeling but some of the leaders as well. We all were silent and very still; you could hear a pin drop as sadness and sorrow filled the room.

My husband was coming to church, but I do not think he was there! He wanted to go after our leader and his partners that took us on a wild goose chase! My husband was still in contact with one of the people that was working with our leader. The man told him he was in Texas and that the money was going to be wired to his account, and he would personally give it to my husband. First, I must say that my husband takes his assignment profoundly serious that he is doing this for God.

He took it personally that the loss of our church and the land was his fault because he is the leader, and ultimately the ball stops with him. We found out sadly to say that other churches were swindled out of money and lost their church as well.

You would think that evil and deceit would not be in the church, but unfortunately, it is. I must say that I am still shocked at the unthinkable things that occur in the Body of Christ. One of my sisters told me that she is shocked proof because she has seen so much! I guess if Judas could walk and talk with Jesus and yet betray Him in His face, then anything is possible.

Looking back at the end of this situation, I would have never thought that after God had poured profusion of favor and blessing on us to get the church with no money down, no proof of who we were, but just with the testimony of the miraculous miracle of my son that keys to a million-dollar property would be given to us and after eight years lose it all because of a scheme and the ruthless of a man of God. We learned many lessons from it all.

After all that we went through, our church is yet going forward, trusting and believing God for greater!

~ Die to Live...~

Turn on the Light!

Jesus is the light. Nothing is brighter than Him. No problem, no sickness, disease, troubled mind, nothing is too dark for Him.

> Can anything [or Who can] separate us from the love Christ has for us? Can troubles [trials; tribulations] or problems [distress; hardship] or sufferings [persecution] or hunger [famine] or nakedness [destitution] or danger or violent death [sword]? But in all these things we are completely victorious through God [or Christ; the One] who showed his love for us. Yes, I am sure [convinced] that neither death, nor life, nor angels, nor ruling spirits [or heavenly rulers; or demons; rulers; principalities], nothing now [in the present], nothing in the future, no powers [or spiritual powers/authorities], nothing above us [or no powers in the sky], nothing below us [or nor powers in the depths], nor anything else in the whole world [any created thing] will ever be able to separate us from the love of God that is in Christ Jesus our Lord.

Romans 8:35, 37-39 (EXB)

Dear reader, whatever we are facing is covered in these passages of scriptures. There is nothing on this earth above or beneath, nothing that can be created that Jesus cannot handle.

Selah...

The problem is do we believe that or not? Do we believe that there is nothing that can separate us from His love?

One of my go-to scriptures is Romans 8:32 (AMP): "He who did not spare [even] His own Son, but gave Him for us all, how will He not also, along with Him, graciously give us all things?"

I have prayed this scripture so many times back to God, and He answered! What can be compared to John 3:16: "God loved us so much that He gave us Jesus!"

Can sickness, financial problems, children, spouses, relationships, jobs, lack, etc., compare? God loves us so much that He is letting us know in His Word, "I got you covered in every area of your life." When we are bombarded with catastrophes and calamities of life, that is when we need to turn the light on. Bring Jesus into our thoughts, into the situation. He is the light, and when the light comes, darkness leaves. As soon as the dark thoughts or situation comes, immediately turn on the light! Do not try to handle the problem all alone; this is when we get into deeper darkness. Remember, the devil comes to steal, kill, and destroy. Let us face it most robbers do not break into a place in the daytime. Robbers wait until it is dark, so no one can see them. They disguised themselves, so they will not be recognized, just like the devil! Satan waits until we let our guards down by trying to handle life and its problems without God. What a big mistake that is to exclude Jesus! When we take Jesus out of the problem, the situation that is when Satan makes his moves. Ephesians 6:12 (EXB) puts it like this:

> [For] Our fight [conflict; struggle] is not against people on earth [flesh and blood] but against the rules and authorities and the powers [or cosmic powers/rulers] of this world's [dark-

ness] against the spiritual powers of evil in the
heavenly world [realm; places].

Ephesians 6:12 (EXB)

Satan is like a professional robber. A professional expert
robber scopes out what they want to steal. They have their focus on the most valuable items. They watch the place they want
to rob for days, months, even years. They watch who comes and
goes. They watch what the target brings in and takes out. They
study the target for a long as it takes to conquer it. Our enemy
is doing the same thing. He is watching us, studying us to see
when the right time for him to break into our life!

We, as Christian, must stay alert! Our souls cannot afford
to linger in a dark place in our life. When you perceive the first
light switch is turned off in the rooms of doom and gloom,
sadness, regret, sorrow, etc., get help! If you do not get help, Satan the robber is watching us, studying us to see when will the
right time to make his move! As soon as he sees the next light
goes out, then the next one, and the next one what happened
the whole house is now dark! Perfect time to break in! Click
on Jesus! Connect to Him immediately!   Ephesians 6:10-
18 (EXB) says that God is strong, and He wants you strong.
So, take everything the master has set out for you, well-made
weapons of the best materials. And put them to use so you will
be able to stand up to everything the devil throws your way.
This is no afternoon athletic contest that we will walk away
from and forget about in a couple of hours. This is for keeps,
a life-or-death fight to the finish against the devil and all his
angels. Be prepared. You are up against far more than you can
handle on your own.

Take all the help you can get, every weapon God has issued,

so that when it's all over but the shouting, you'll still be on your feet. Truth, righteousness, peace, faith, and salvation are more than words. Learn how to apply them. You'll need them throughout your life. God's Word is an *indispensable* weapon. In the same way, prayer is essential in this ongoing warfare. Pray hard and long. Pray for your brothers and sisters. Keep your eyes open. Keep each other's spirits up so that no one falls behind or drops out.

Darkness

I was told by my cousin, a soldier, that when he was over in Iraq, it was so dark that they could not see anything! Just black, thick darkness! This kind of darkness makes me think how dark hell is. What a horrifying place! The soldier said it was the most frightful time in his life. I cannot imagine being in the total absences of light! The sad thing is that people who refuse to accept Jesus Christ as Savior are in absence of the light. My pastor said this profound statement that I will never forget, "Living in hell is like living in total darkness with *no feel of life*!" he said not only will there be gnashing of teeth, indescribable pain but no life! Nothing will be connected to life.

Selah...

But there is hope! If a person is alive, they still have the opportunity to give their life to Christ and not only receive the light but become a light in this dark world. Hallelujah! It is magnificent to know that no matter how dark your situation is, it is not too dark for God. God can find you at the midnight of your life. No matter how dark or blacker than black it is, God can find you and help you.

~ Die to Live... ~

Glow in the Dark

In the beginning [before all time] was the Word (Christ), and the Word was with God, and the Word was God Himself. He was [continually existing] in the beginning [co-eternally] with God. All things were made *and* came into existence through Him; and without Him not even one thing was made that has come into being. In Him was life [and the power to bestow life], and the life was the Light of men. The Light shines on in the darkness, and the darkness did not understand it *or* overpower it *or* appropriate it *or* absorb it [and is unreceptive to it].

John 1:1-5 (AMP)

I heard my son's headmaster at his school say these words as he was addressing the senior class, "Glow in the dark." Those four words stood out to me as I visualized shining like a beacon light for Christ.

As I thought about glowing in the dark, I see myself as wanting to be a glow stick. It is translucent, luminous, and radiant! The glow stick glows the brightest in the dark, and if you think about it, what is the use for it in the light? What good is it if we just glow in the church if we are trying to win souls? How is that helping someone in the dark to see? The world is a dark room full of souls that need to see the light. How can they see our light if we will not shine when we are around them or will not go where they are at? We cannot afford to dim our lights or turn our lights off when we are around darkness just to fit in for that moment. What if that moment is the perfect opportunity to witness or pray for a person that just might be suicidal? Some people are looking for the light, looking for hope, and looking for words of encouragement. Why not let it be you?

~ Die to Live... ~

We Need the Light to See

When we are in the dark, and you are trying to find something, one of the first things we look for to use is a flashlight. Why? Because we cannot see. We need some light to find what we are looking for. Some people are looking for an answer to their emptiness. We can be flashlights shining bright, leading people to Jesus Christ!

Lights draw people to it. What is a Christmas tree without lights? Just a tree with ornaments. We do not just want to be a Christian with just ornaments (our gifts and talents); we want to be lit! We want our lights to shine through the ornaments to draw souls to the light, which is Christ!

Glow for Jesus

If we want our light to shine brighter to be an incandescent glow stick, we must go through the heat. An incandescent light containing a filament that glows white-hot when heated. Unfortunately, we do not like to go through trials and tribulations, but it is the heat the fire of the situation that brings us closer to God, causing the beast of the flesh to melt. Without being tried, we will not come out like pure gold.

Glow Even in Sadness

One night as I laid next to my love, my husband, I looked at him wrapped in pain, and soft tears began to fall gently down my face, for my heart was sadden in my soul. My pillow was soaked with I need thee. I began to pray, asking God to remember us and to have mercy. As I began to thank God and give Him praise, I said: "Father, I just don't want to glow in the dark in front of people, but I want to glow in the dark private times in my life and when I am at war with the beauty and the Beast-N-Me." I want to glow when I am being beaten down or under attack, and no one is around but me. I want to glow! I want the light of Christ to shine until the dark situation is captured and seized by the glory of God!

Sometimes our greatest test is when we are alone! I encourage you to glow! Glow in your praise! Glow in your worship! The radiance of Christ will come to your situation, and transformation will take place! The light of the world is inside of you, and His name is Jesus! Praise Him!

~ Die to Live…~

The Light's Purpose

Matthew 5:13-16 (MSG) blew my mind! It says:

Let me tell you why you are here. You're here to
be salt-seasoning that brings out the God-flavors
of this earth. If you lose your saltiness, how will
people taste godliness? You've lost your useful-
ness and will end up in the garbage. Here's another way to put it: You're here to be light, bringing out the God-colors in the world. God is not a
secret to be kept. We're going public with this, as
public as a city on a hill. If I make you light-bear-
ers, you don't think I'm going to hide you under a
bucket, do you? I'm putting you on a light stand.
Now that I've put you there on a hilltop, on a
light stand—shine! Keep open house; be generous with your lives. By opening up to others,
you'll prompt people to open up with God, this
generous Father in heaven.

Don't Allow Your Day to Be Useless

The Word! The Word! The Word! Okay, this is what got
me! If we do not live right for God, if we do not let our light
shine, we will lose our saltiness and will not be good for anything, just useless! It is no wonder it is a dark world, so many
of the lights of Christ the glow sticks are gone dim or simply
been put out.

After reading this translation, I told my church and have
added this in my prayers that I don't want God to throw not
one day of my life in the garbage and say, "You wasted my day,
this day adds up to nothing, I have no use for this day. This day
is added up to naught! Nothing! *Wow*! How sad is that?"

Another sad thing is that we, as Christian in general, have

the audacity to keep God a secret! There are so many other religious groups that are bold about their god, they go door to door, sell pies in suits in ninety-degree weather, etc., but where are the Christians? Why do we have to be quiet and shut up about our God? It seems as if all other religions have freedom of speech but Christians. I know that there are many Christians that are bold for Jesus Christ, but there are too many that are not. I remember hearing a message from the late Dr. Myles Monroe, and he said, "If there is nothing to Christianity, then why are so many religions threaten by it?"

I often wondered why if we are a Christian nation, then why can't we pray in schools? It should at least be an option. I remember working in a Christian childcare facility and one of the children was a Jehovah's witness. One day another child had a birthday and was celebrating her party in the class. We were told because of her religion that the child was not allowed to attend the party and had to sit outside the classroom and read a book or play. The child was not to participate at all, we could not even give her a cookie. The same thing happened at Christmas. I did not understand why a parent would send their child to a Christian school that they did not agree with the doctrine of that school. My point is that the parents were given an option. Why can't we be given an option to pray if we want to or not? We cannot say Jesus in our prayers on our jobs, in ceremonies, speeches; we cannot celebrate Christmas in public it has to be happy holidays or Santa. The Nativity scene is gone! The world has X-Mas Jesus right out of His day! There would not be a Christmas without Christ! If Jesus had not come, there would be no such thing as Christmas trees, gifts, toys, Santa, or his reindeers! Some workers that work in stores have told me it's upsetting to them that they can't say, "Merry Christmas," but they can say happy Halloween, etc. and now some Christian churches won't even say the name of Jesus anymore less preach about Jesus; how sad is that! God, help us! The devil is loving this; he knows that there is power in the name of *Jesus*! He knows Jesus is the Savior of the world! He just does not want anyone to be saved. He wants as many souls as possible to go to hell with him. Jesus, Jesus, Jesus!

Remember,

> You are the light of [Christ to] the world. A city set on a hill cannot be hidden; nor does *anyone* light a lamp and put it under a basket, but on a lampstand, and it gives light to all who are in the house. Let your light shine before men in such a way that they may see your good deeds *and* moral excellence, and [recognize and honor and] glorify your Father who is in heaven.
>
> Matthew 5:14-16 (AMP)

Father, help us to be luminous and shine like the stars in the sky on this earth for Your glory in Jesus's name.

~ Die to Live… ~

The Beastly Spirit Exposed

Identify—the distinguishing character or personality of an individual; establish or indicate who or what (someone or something) is.

> For our struggle is not against flesh and blood [contending only with physical opponents], but against the rulers, against the powers, against the world forces of this [present] darkness, against the spiritual *forces* of wickedness in the heavenly (supernatural) *places*.
>
> Ephesians 6:12 (AMP)

> [For] Our fight [conflict; struggle] is not against people on earth [flesh and blood] but against the rulers and authorities and the powers [*or* cosmic powers/rulers] of this world's darkness [darkness], against the spiritual powers of evil in the heavenly world [realm; places].
>
> Ephesians 6:12 (EXB)

> For we are not fighting against people made of flesh and blood, but against persons without bodies—the evil rulers of the unseen world, those mighty satanic beings and great evil princes of darkness who rule this world; and against huge numbers of wicked spirits in the spirit world.
>
> Ephesians 6:12 (TLB)

Know Your Component

Our fight is not against flesh and blood, but we are fighting against spirits of wickedness. This is a serious fight because, as humans, we fight against what we can see. We cannot see spirits, just the effects of them. For us to defeat the enemy, the evil one, we must have the Holy Spirit and know that only with God's Spirit can we win. We will never win in our own strength! We must stay alert and stay on the lookout for the evil spirits that are seeking someone to devour.

The BS, beastly spirit must die! The flesh is where evil spirits try to hide out. They hint and suggest things to the BS that will oppose or offend God. Once again, we must have the Holy Spirit. Evil spirits cannot infiltrate the Holy Spirit! They cannot subvert God! Evil spirits know that the flesh is in a war against the Holy Spirit, and they will try to assist the flesh as much as possible!

Look at this world we live in. The power of the BS, the flesh, is being activated and used by evil spirits. It is not God's will that people go into schools and shoot children and the faculty. It is not of God that the beastly spirit is in our homes being seen through disobedient children, fighting husbands and wives, drugs and alcohol taking over, and suicides are at an all-time high. Since when did road rage get so violent that drivers will follow a person to their home, get out of their car and shoot them just because they cut in front of them! Really! People are driving like maniacs! In and out of traffic and speeding like crazy while giving someone the middle finger! We have seen on the news just because of someone's race or religion, someone just drove up and killed them! The beast has lost it! Look at this world and all the wars! We can clearly identify the Beastly Spirit working overtime all over the world! Remember, the beastly spirit is difficult to control and hard to deal with. If you want to see the BS in action, just turn on the news, and we see the *Beastly Spirit*! We see robbery, rape, liars, murders, we see the dishonesty, racism, social injustice is at an all-time high! We see discrimination, ageism and homophobia, xenophobia, sexism, chauvinism, and you name it—we are experiencing it!

The beastly spirit is everywhere! In our government, we see congress against the senate, in the school's principals, teachers, and the children can't work together. The home is in chaos! Where there is turmoil, madness, and confusion, you can find the BS, the beastly spirit, in action. We thank God there is hope! That hope is in Jesus Christ.

The BS Exposed in the Home and Family

War has been declared on the family! The BS has taken over because the parents are no longer in the home! So many children have to raise themselves. The home is lacking a good structure base. That base is God, love, consistency, support, and discipline. Who is teaching the children? Who is our future? Who is teaching them the world's conflict resolution! They will not know how to calmly come together and work things out or learn how to share. This is the breeding place for the beastly spirit. It is sad to say, but so many of our children are lost or displaced. There has never been a time in the history of America that there is such a massive disconnect. The separation begins when parents no longer have time for their children, their home, or family. I can use one word that has caused this separation "busy" everybody is too busy for one another. Here we see the (BS) beastly spirit again, *self*! It's all about me, my career, my wants and desires, my friends, my social life, my fitness, and the list can go on. The disconnection begins slowly and slowly until parents do not know their own child anymore.

Looking at the family, we can see how transparent the disconnect is. How can a parent not see that their child is troubled when they disconnect themselves from the family! How cannot a parent see depression all over the child's face or actions! How can a parent not know something is wrong when your child will not eat, stay in their room, start dressing out of their character, or start hanging out with trouble! How can a parent not see their child experimenting with drugs, alcohol, and sex unless there is a disconnection? How can you see something that is detectable but you do not see it? The answer is easy, "No one is home!" Or in some cases, the parents are home, but their mind is not there. Just too busy on the phone or social media, and watching tv, etc.

Parents will not know unless they spend quality time!

Unfortunately, it appears that some people want to stay in a five-star hotel but live in a one-star home. The simple solution is to prioritize the time from the most important thing in your life to the least. In my opinion, God is first, then family.

The family should always be a high priority because they are a part of you. Don't you want the best for yourself? If so, we should want the best for our family. Whatever we invest in, that is where we are going to see the results. Spend quality time with your family. Value their words, smiles, funny jokes, actions, and questions, etc. Time is precious and priceless. Once it is gone, we cannot redeem it back. Cherish every moment.

Home Remedy

If you want a home where the beastly spirit cannot live, then pull out the recipe book! If we want our children to behave, the recipe says, "Point your kids in the right direction— when they are old, they won't be lost" (Proverbs 22:6, MSG). The Word of God has all recipes for everything in life.

Think what it would be like if homes were based on God, His Word, and His principles. Homes would be enriched with love, harmony, consideration, peace, the family would be taught that love is not selfish, and sharing is caring.

We would see an increase in church attendance, helping people, being kind, working together, having fun, and lots of laughter!

The Home is the Foundation

I believe the home is the foundation. How we think and act has a lot to do with how we were raised. You can almost tell what kind of home a child is coming from by the way they talk and behave. How they model respect, how they set boundaries, and how discipline had been administered.

One thing to remember is that actions speak louder than words. What goes on in the home behind closed doors will come out when the door is opened.

God Is Love

The Excellence of Love:

> If I speak with the tongues of men and of angels, but have not love [for others growing out of God's love for me], then I have become only a noisy gong or a clanging cymbal [just an annoying distraction]. And if I have *the gift of* prophecy

[and speak a new message from God to the people], and understand all mysteries, and [possess] all knowledge; and if I have all [sufficient] faith so that I can remove mountains, but do not have love [reaching out to others], I am nothing. If I give all my possessions to feed *the poor*, and if I surrender my body to be burned, but do not have love, it does me no good at all. Love endures with patience *and* serenity, love is kind *and* thoughtful, and is not jealous *or* envious; love does not brag and is not proud *or* arrogant. It is not rude; it is not self-seeking; it is not provoked [nor overly sensitive and easily angered]; it does not take into account a wrong *endured*. It does not rejoice at injustice but rejoices with the truth [when right and truth prevail]. Love bears all things [regardless of what comes], believes all things [looking for the best in each one], hopes all things [remaining steadfast during difficult times], endures all things [without weakening]. Love never fails [it never fades nor ends].

1 Corinthians 13:1-8 (AMP)

We always hear, "Love is what it does" how true this saying is. The MSG said in verse seven, "So, no matter what I say, what I believe, and what I do, I'm bankrupt without love."

Gobsmacked! Bankrupt! We are empty and barren without *love*. That is like an

ocean without water or a woman that is pregnant having all the symptoms, her stomach is protruding out, but it is empty inside! No baby! Without *love,* everything is meaningless.

A House Filled with Love

Let love fill your home with beautiful decorations of compliments and praise. Use the paint as helping one another out, the primer as corrective criticism, and all the furniture can be the representation of equipping everyone with what they need. Make sure you have the doors of forgiveness hung, then open the windows of praise so the fragrant of God's aroma will fill the house with love. The warmth of love will be shown every day and all throughout the year! How wonderful it would be to have a united front tied together with the strongest glue that Satan cannot evaporate, and that is the love of God!

It Is Okay, to Be Honest

I have heard parents say when their child is misbehaving, "*Oh,* isn't he or she so cute" or just ignore the behavior in hopes that it will go away. My pastor once said that all the people in jail or prison were somebody's sweet little baby. It is probably hard to phantom that during their sweet little lives, the parent probably never would have thought that their child would end up that way. Parents must take on the responsibility no matter how hard it is to discipline in the right way.

The Bible says, "The truth will make you free. The truth is simply being honest, and dealing with reality, facing the fact and the veracity of what you see and hear." When the truth is told, it will help form and establish a person. When telling the truth to your child, it will help shape their mind from wrong thinking, therefore, affecting their actions and decisions. The truth is children are children and not adults. This is something else my pastor taught, "Stop expecting a child to make an adult decision." Is it fair to put that kind of pressure on a child to think like an adult? Think like someone that has been on the earth for over twenty-five to fifty years or however old the parent might be? Let us face it sometimes we as an adult have a hard time making the right decision. I work with children, and I see it all the time when one kid says, "I want the purple paint," then all the kids want the purple paint. We could be watching a commercial and McDonald's come on showing a happy meal. Mom walks in the door and asks the child what do they want for dinner? The child immediately says, "McDonald's!" Why? Because that is what they just saw. They do not even think about it. Their minds are so impressionable and immature. You can ask a child if they want some vegetables or cookies, and we all know what the answer is going to be—"Cookies!" They do not know what is best for them. That is why they need adult parents to lead and guide them. We understand it is all about choice, but when the choice is above their pay grade, do not feel bad that you had to step in and make the choice for them. Remember, you are the investor!

The BS Exposed in Bullying

We as a nation are experiencing bullying like we never have in the history of America. Here we see the beastly spirit in full control. The bully has a beastly spirit! If we look at all the bullies, we see that they are difficult to control or deal with! If we take a close look into their homes, we will probably see the beastly spirit attitude of a contemptible, vile, hateful person difficult to control or deal with.

Merriam Webster defines bullying as abuse and mistreatment of someone vulnerable by someone stronger, more powerful, acts or written or spoken words intended to intimidate or harass a person or to cause physical harm to a person or his or her property.

This bully BS is so strong that children as young as seven years old are committing suicide over what someone has said or done. No longer can we ignore the signs just because of the child's age. If a teacher, a friend, or family member, etc., tells a parent that their child is acting a certain way, they should not take it for grant it. The Bible tells us to watch and pray! When I use the word watch, I mean watch what the child is doing, who they are hanging out with, what kinds of music and movies they are watching. Check out their Facebook page, all their social media accounts. See if they are eating or not, how they respond to you in an answer. Listen to the tone of voice they use, their actions, and the attitudes they display. Observe if they want to be left alone a lot, isolated from everyone, these are some signs that something is going on, and attention to this matter is required.

There has never been a time in my life I have seen so many mean children, adults, young and old. During my generation, we would not have the audacity to talk to our parents in a crazy way, display such a foul, offensive, and horrible attitude to our parents or any adults.

If you are experiencing someone bullying you, please go to your parents, a teacher, guidance counselor an adult that you can trust. Do not take it for grant it. This is profoundly serious. Let us put a stop to bullying. Signs are there if we would just take a closer look.

We see the BS in our workplaces, hospitals, and nursing homes; it is even in our churches! The beastly spirit can be seen from the pulpit to the last row. Wherever you see pastors and leaders refusing to allow God's will, God's way be done, you see the BS! When churches refuse to let the Holy Spirit rest, rule, abide, and direct, you see the BS in action! The beast always wants its way.

This is God's kingdom, and He needs to be king! Haven't you seen pastors and leaders that will not at hear to anyone, not even God? It is either their way or no way, they want it to be all about them. This is the BS in control. Sometimes I wonder how in the world could anyone think they know more than the Creator of the world. How can we tell God how to run His business which is kingdom business? It is not only the pastors and leaders—some members are guilty as well. When the pastor and leaders give godly directions to the congregation, and they do not follow, that is the BS. We need to pray for the pastors who must deal with the BS, which is difficult, hardheaded, stubbornly hard to deal with people. In Exodus 32:9 (AMP), Moses had to deal with the BS. The scripture said, "The Lord said to Moses, 'I have seen these people, and behold, they are a stiff-necked (stubborn, rebellious) people.'"

I think we all have encountered someone like this and even within our self. We see this kind of behavior all the time, and it is getting worse! There is nothing new under the sun. The same spirits that were roaming around in the Bible days are still roaming around today. No new demons or spirits are being made. One thing that is so amazing about God is that He has given us the way out of any and everything, and that includes our actions and thoughts.

> No temptation [regardless of its source] has overtaken *or* enticed you that is not common to human experience [nor is any temptation unusual or beyond human resistance]; but God is faithful [to His word—He is compassionate and trustworthy], and He will not let you be tempted beyond your ability [to resist], but along with the temptation He

[has in the past and is now and] will [always] provide the way out as well, so that you will be able to endure it [without yielding, and will overcome temptation with joy].

1 Corinthians 10:13 (AMP)

Reading this scripture, God is letting us know that there is no enticement that we cannot resist. Not even if someone is giving you the doldrums, giving you the business, you have God's power within you to hold your peace, not go off, control your attitude and respond in a manner that Jesus would. All enticements are not limited to just sex, drugs, and alcohol. There are so many ways enticements, offers, invitations, baits, and attractions come our way.

Let us look at 1 Corinthians 10:13 (MSG):

No test or temptation that comes your way is beyond the course of what others have had to face. All you need to remember is that God will never let you down; he'll never let you be pushed past your limit; he'll always be there to help you come through it.

1 Corinthians 10:13 (MSG)

The only temptations that you have are the same temptations that all people have. But you can trust God. He will not let you be tempted more than you can bear. But when you are tempted, God will also give you a way to escape that temptation. Then you will be able to endure it.

Satan loves the BS, the beastly spirit, because he knows that spirit is a hindrance to the church and the body of Christ. Satan loves it when the flesh is doing what it wants to do because that is where he operates. He knows that when self, flesh, the BS is out front, he has the opportunity to be in control.

> But I need something *more*! For if I know the law but still can't keep it, and if the power of sin within me keeps sabotaging my best intentions, I obviously need help! I realize that I don't have what it takes. I can will it, but I can't *do* it. I decide to do good, but I don't *really* do it; I decide not to do bad, but then I do it anyway. My decisions, such as they are, don't result in actions. Something has gone wrong deep within me and gets the better of me every time.

Romans 7:18-20 (MSG)

The enemy loves it when the big "I" is in control because there is no room for anyone else, not even God.

"For I know that nothing good dwells within me, that is, in my flesh. I can will what is right, but I cannot perform it. [I have the intention and urge to do what is right, but no power to carry it out.]" (AMPC)

~ Die to Live… ~

The Hostile Beast

Evil in the Land ~ The Beast Is at Work!

What a serious critical alarming, distressing time we are living in. Trouble is everywhere. Trouble in the home, schools, workplace, churches, the streets, from the lowest place to the highest we can find trouble, trouble, trouble all over the world! We see chaos to a degree we have never seen before! The decay of this world is because of human beings. Corruption did not come from God; this is a human invention. It has never been a time like what we are seeing and experiencing. I was told an alarming thing in my young walk in Christ and have never forgotten this statement "Christians are the only army that kills its own soldiers!" How sad is that! We all have one enemy, and that is the devil, and we have the nerves to fight each other! We see churches against churches, denominations against denominations, worship styles against worship styles, etc.! Evil, evil, evil is everywhere!

When has it ever been that a person would walk into a church with no mask or disguised and kill without any remorse! If anything, they use to respect the House of God but no more! There is no doubt about it, we need our Lord and Savior Jesus Christ! We need help! Rescue us Almighty God from desolations of evil in Jesus's name. The Bible has told us about perilous, dangerous, and terrifying times and what to expect. Well, it is here! We are in it! We see it, we read about it, and even experience it. The Bible is rhema! Everything we need to know is in the Word of God. Let us sharpen our sword (the Bible) like never before by reading it, believing it, and living it out because the fight is on!

For the word of God is quick, and powerful,
and sharper than any two-edged sword, piercing

even to the dividing asunder of soul and spirit,
and of the joints and marrow, and is a discerner
of the thoughts and intents of the heart.

Hebrews 4:12 (KJV)

For the word of God is living and active *and*
full of power [making it operative, energizing,
and effective]. It is sharper than any two-edged
[b]sword, penetrating as far as the division of the
[c]soul and spirit [the completeness of a person],
and of both joints and marrow [the deepest parts
of our nature], exposing *and* judging the very
thoughts and intentions of the heart.

Hebrews 4:12 (AMP)

*Thank you, Father, for making a way for us to live without
fear and preparing us for the right now.*

*We must stay in the Word of God and be attentive to
His Voice.*

~ Die to Live...~

The Root of the World's Deterioration

Evil in the land, the beast is at work! I was praying and asking God, "Why is it so much anger and hate in the world?" God told me to read Romans the seventh chapter, and I would see the root of it all, which is *sin.*

This little three-letter word "sin" is small, but it is so *big* and powerful! This three-letter word has caused the worst things you can think of to happen, even death, and what is even more horrendous is so powerful that it causes eternal death.

> We are all infected and impure with sin. When we display our righteous deeds, they are nothing but filthy rags. Like autumn leaves, we wither and fall, and our sins sweep us away like the wind.
>
> Isaiah 64:6 (NLT)

Thank God there is help through our Lord and Savior Jesus Christ!

> We know that the Law is spiritual, but I am *a creature* of the flesh [worldly, self-reliant—carnal and unspiritual], sold into slavery to sin [and serving under its control]. For I do not understand my own actions [I am baffled and bewildered by them]. I do not practice what I want *to do*, but I am doing the very thing I hate [and yielding to my human nature, my worldliness—my sinful capacity]. Now if I *habitually* do what I do not want to do, [that means] I agree with the Law, *confessing* that it is good (morally excellent). So now [if that is the case, then]

it is no longer I who do it [the disobedient thing which I despise], but the sin [nature] which lives in me. For I know that nothing good lives in me, that is, in my flesh [my human nature, my worldliness—my sinful capacity]. For the willingness [to do good] is present in me, but the doing of good is not. For the good that I want to do, I do not do, but I practice the very evil that I do not want. But if I am doing the very thing I do not want to do, I am no longer the one doing it [that is, it is not me that acts], but the sin [nature] which lives in me.

So I find *it to be* the law [of my inner self], that evil is present in me, the one who wants to do good. For I joyfully delight in the law of God in my inner self [with my new nature], but I see a different law *and* rule of action in the members of my body [in its appetites and desires], waging war against the law of my mind *and* subduing me and making me a prisoner of the law of sin which is within my members.

Romans 7:14-23 (AMP)

For I do not understand my own actions [I am baffled and bewildered by them]. I do not practice what I want to do, but I am doing the very thing I hate [and yielding to my human nature, my worldliness—my sinful capacity].

Romans 7:15 (AMP)

~ Die to Live… ~

Enslaved by the Beast

Galatians 5:1 (NKJV): "Stand fast therefore in the liberty by which Christ has made us free, and do not be entangled again with a yoke of bondage."

Slave defined—one that is completely subservient to a dominating influence; held in or forced into servitude: *enslaved.*

When I hear the word slave, it is not a good picture that comes to my mind. No one wants to be a slave to another person. What I think is worst than being a slave to a person is being a slave to the devil! Jesus has freed us from the slave master of sin. Why would we want to go back into it? The BS, the beast, gets itself entangled and intertwine in sin. The beast is something to reckon with! Just the thought of being a slave or imprisoned, yoked, and confined to the devil makes me speechless. The BS, beastly spirit is blind, sightless to the wilds of the devil. Remember, the flesh has a sinful nature, a sinful spirit and, a sinful personality, and a sinful attitude.

God has given us power through the Holy Spirit to continue to live free from sin. Therefore, we do not need to entangle ourselves in sinful things that cause death.

First Corinthians 6:11 (AMP) helps us by saying:

> And such were some of you [before you believed]. But you were washed [by the atoning sacrifice of Christ], you were sanctified [set apart for God, and made holy], you were justified [declared free of guilt] in the name of the Lord Jesus Christ and in the [Holy] Spirit of our God [the source of the believer's new life and changed behavior].

1 Corinthians 6:11 (AMP)

Now that we have a changed behavior; and have been set apart for God through Jesus, why go back into what is not good, back into a sinful life? God has made us holy for Himself. First Peter 1:16 (ERV) says: "In the Scriptures, God says, 'Be holy, because I am holy.'" God has made a way for us to live a holy life through Jesus having His Holy Spirit to equip us in our everyday living.

> Christ set us free so that we could live in freedom [to a place of freedom; *or* by means of freedom;]. So, stand strong. Do not change and go back into the slavery of the law [submit/be fastened to a yoke of slavery].

Galatians 5:1 (EXB)

The BS our flesh fights us against holy living. I ask the question, "Why sell yourself back into slavery?" Christ has set us free.

> Try to live in [Pursue] peace with all people, and try to live free from sin [pursue holiness/sanctification]. [For] Anyone whose life is not holy [sanctified] will never see the Lord.

Hebrews 12:14 (EXB)

Whatever we do, please, *stay free*!

Freedom Brings on Tranquility

Freedom is contagious. When Harriette Tubman was freed, she wanted to free others. The autonomy she must have felt! Harriette experienced such a phenomenal relief that she was determined for other slaves to experience it as well! The relief and release of mental and physical chains that had her bound were off! For the first time in her life, she experienced tranquility, she finally had an awareness of what peace was. Can you imagine living in fear and turmoil, not knowing when your door would be busted down, and the owner of you could come in and rape you or kill you anytime they wanted to? The stress of fear is enough all by itself, not along with all the other hideous and revolting things that could occur.

Well, there is still a slave master, and his name is Satan! He is worse than any human slave master could ever be! He does not care who you are, how old you are, and where you came from, what church you go to, or if you do not go! He does not care if you are a believer or a non-believer! He has one goal, and that is to take you to hell with him! He is the cruelest of cruel mastering over people who refuse to give their life to Christ. He will bust down the doors of your life and rob you of all your goods! Rob you from your peace, joy, and happiness, your purpose, and your plans! He will rape you from your hopes and dreams and leave you laying in the blood of human despair! His chains are heavy! Heavy with guilt and shame! His whips are tied together with lies that you are nothing and God does not love you! He beats people every day with negativity, the give-ups, quit you can't do it, cheat no one will find out, steal you can keep it, kill people do it every day, commit suicide no one loves you! He is the master of lies.

> You are of *your* father the devil, and it is your will to practice the desires [which are characteristic] of your father. He was a murderer from the beginning and does not stand in the truth because there is no truth in him. When he lies, he speaks what is natural to him, for he is a liar and the father of lies *and* half-truths.
>
> John 8:44 (AMP)

The devil is no good! There is no good in him! He *hates* us because he *hates God!* He hates the fact that God loves us so much that He gave us Jesus, and now we are His children. He hates that we will get to live with God, and he will never ever get that opportunity again to live in heaven. It is time to get off the plantation of sin and death and live in the land of freedom. If you have given your life to Christ, stay free! If you have not, this is a good time to receive freedom through Christ Jesus.

Romans 10:9-11 (EXB) tells us how:

> If you declare [confess] with your mouth, "Jesus is Lord," and if you believe in your heart that God raised Jesus from the dead, you will be saved. [For] We believe with our hearts, and so we are made right with God [are justified; receive righteousness]. And we declare [confess] with our mouths, and so we are saved [leading to salvation]. As the Scripture says, "Anyone who trusts [believes] in him will never be disappointed [*or* put to shame]."
>
> Romans 10:9-11 (EXB)

Steps to Salvation:

Ask God to forgive you for all sins.

Ask God to come and dwell in your heart.

Ask God to fill you with His Holy Spirit.

Ask God to give you a desire to seek Him and give you an understanding of His Word.

Start off reading the book of John.

Pray without ceasing.

Join a church that teaches the truth of the Word of God.

Be faithful.

I am praying for you, and welcome to the family of Christ!

If you need more help with the plan of salvation, you can email me at…or go to your local churches in your area that are Bible-based.

The Weight of Sin

I cannot imagine how Harriette Tubman must have felt being beaten, worked like a mule, and only getting to eat slop and the leftovers. I can only compare or try to relate my life to her life when I was living in the bondage of sin. The weight of sin is so heavy. Sin can weigh you down to the point that some people are crushed by it, and they never get all those weights off, and they die in bondage. That is so sad because Jesus is the lifter of our soul, and there is nothing not-a-thing that is too heavy for Him. Praise Him!

When I gave my life to Christ, the freedom from the weight of sin was lifted off from me like a ton of bricks! It felt like I was dragging around bricks everywhere I went. Bricks tied to my legs, arms, mind, and my heart. Don't' get me wrong, sin has its pleasures, but there is a deadly price to it! When I would get to myself, I felt the weight of the sin! I felt dirty and used! The slave master of sin did not care how I felt afterward. The devil is a user, and he wants to use anyone that lets him until he uses them to death! I believe sin is a spirit. It is the spirit that is within a person that causes them to sin. The devil is not walking around telling us to do this or that as if he was a person. He is a spirit. If a person does not have the Holy Spirit, the sinful nature that we were born in is familiar and attractive to the sin spirit causing a person to be willing to commit sin without reservation.

Jesus said, "I tell you most solemnly that anyone who chooses a life of sin is trapped in a dead-end life and is, in fact, a slave. A slave is a transient, who can't come and go at will. The Son, though, has an established position, the run of the house. So if the Son sets you free, you are free through and through. I know you are Abraham's descendants. But I also know that you are trying to kill me because my message hasn't yet penetrated your thick skulls. I'm talking about things I have seen while keeping company with the Father, and you just go on doing what you have heard from your father."

John 8:34-35 (MSG)

We do not have to be enslaved and imprisoned by the devil any longer. We have been given a name change! In slavery days, when you became free, you had the opportunity to change your name. Now that we have given our lives to Christ, we get to change our names from sinner to saint, from alcoholic to sober, from a liar to truth-teller, from dirty to clean, from hating to loving everyone, from strife to peace, from doubter to believer and the list goes on. Whatever you used to be, you are no longer that anymore. We have been given freedom through Jesus Christ to live a victorious life here on this earth.

Thank you, Jesus, for freeing us from the bondage of sin!

"So If the Son makes you free, then you are unquestionably free" (John 8:36, AMP).

~ Die to Live…~

Deception

The Deceived Beast

You [O] foolish [stupid] Galatians! Who has tricked [*or* cast a spell on; bewitched] you? You were told very clearly about the death of Jesus Christ on the cross [Before your eyes Jesus Christ was publicly portrayed/announced as crucified]. Tell me this one thing: How did you receive the Holy Spirit? Did you receive the Spirit by following [the works of] the law? No, you received the Spirit [...or] because you heard the Good News and believed it [by believing what you heard]. Are you so foolish [How can you be so stupid]? You began your life in Christ by [by; *or* through] the Spirit. Now are you trying to make it complete [finish; *or* be perfected] by your own power [human effort; the flesh]? Were all your experiences wasted [*or* Have you suffered so much for nothing]? I hope not [*or* Surely it was not for nothing;—if indeed for nothing]! Does God give you the Spirit and work miracles among you because you follow [by the works of] the law? No, he does these things [...or] because you heard the Good News and believed it [by your believing what you heard].

Galatians 3:1-5 (EXB)

Deceive defined—to cause to accept as true or valid what is false or invalid

(Merriam Webster).

Another definition is (of a person) cause (someone) to believe something that is not true, typically in order to gain some personal advantage. Synonyms: swindle defraud cheat trick hoodwink hoax dupe take in mislead delude fool outwit misguide lead on inveigle seduce ensnare entrap beguile double-cross gull con bamboozle do sting gyp diddle fiddle swizzle rip off shaft bilk rook pull a fast one on pull someone's leg take for a ride pull the wool over someone's eyes throw dust in someone's eyes put one over on.

You are probably wondering why I listed all these synonyms. Just reading them, I have experienced deception throughout my life, sometimes from people that were the closest to me. Deception is one of Satan's greatest strategies. Keep your eyes open because deception is everywhere and the spirit of deception is prevalent and persistent; we do not have to be bamboozled ever again.

Hoodwinked

The devil uses temptation to lure the BS, flesh into sin to bring forth death.

> But people are [each person is] tempted when their own evil desire leads [lures; drags] them away and traps [entices; lures] them. This desire leads to sin [Then, after desire is conceived, it gives birth to sin], and

then the sin grows [*or* becomes full-grown] and
brings [gives birth to] death.

James 1:14-15 (EXB)

God has made a way in every area of our lives to live a life
pleasing to Him. I must say again, "This is the fight of our life,
and the devil does not fight fair!" The devil can be referred to
as a "pimp." Just like a pimp, he baits you by dangling things in
front of you that you like trying to seduce you. If it is power, he
dingles power, if it is men or women, money, fame, etc., he dingles that too. He lures you in by giving you gifts and pleasur-
able things, then, once he has you in his power, he puts you out
on the street of life and uses you up until you are drained from
the abuse of sin! And that's not all, just like a pimp beating his
prostitute, the devil begins to beat you, and he keeps beating
you and beating you with harmful words, "You are nothing, nobody likes or loves you," "you will never mount up to anything,"
he torments and plagues you with sickness or disease, then bad
things start happening to you one after another! Then he has
the nerves, the boldness to tell you that he loves you! Madness!
How can the devil love! He does not love anyone! He is the
opposite of love! He knows he is dammed forever, and he just
wants to get as many people to be dammed with him!

I confess that I was a fool! Crazy! Deceived, duped, the
wool was pulled over my eyes! I fell into the traps of the devil! I
grew up in a home where my father was a pastor and my mother was an evangelist. I knew that just because my parents were
saved did not mean that I was saved. At the age of twelve years
old, I gave my life to Christ with an understanding of what
salvation meant. I remember my sister and I had come home
from a revival where the preacher showed a video on hell. After

the video was over, the preacher taught about salvation and the Holy Spirit, we both said we wanted to be saved and filled with the power of God. When we got home, we wanted more of the Holy Spirit! We began to pray, asking God to fill us! Before we knew it, we were crying out, calling on Jesus! Right before our eyes, the room changed! The room was filled with the anointing and the glory of God! There was no doubt about it the presence of God was there! The room was so bright! It was as if we were standing inside the middle of the sun! I have never seen a brightness like that before in my life! The presence of God was so prevalent in the room that my mother and other family members came in the room to see what was going on. We both were speaking in tongues, the heavenly language! We experienced Pentecost from Acts 2:1-4 (AMP):

> When the day of Pentecost had come, they were all together in one place, and suddenly a sound came from heaven like a rushing violent wind, and it filled the whole house where they were sitting. There appeared to them tongues resembling fire, which were being distributed [among them], and they rested on each one of them [as each person received the Holy Spirit]. And they were all filled [that is, diffused throughout their being] with the Holy Spirit and began to speak in other tongues (different languages), as the Spirit was giving them the ability to speak out [clearly and appropriately].

Acts 2:1-4 (AMP)

I understand why speaking in tongues is referred to as a

heavenly language because, in our humanness, we cannot explain it. We can only interpret the heavenly language through the Holy Spirit.

My sister, being only fourteen years old, began prophesying and laying on hands. God began to use us at our young age. At the age of twelve, because of being filled with the Holy Spirit, I was appointed the president of one of the ministries called the "Sunshine Band," which is children ages three to twelve. Normally this position is for adults. I had no idea that this was the beginning of one of my purposes in life which I am still actively working in now for over thirty years, and that is working with children. I only wished that my father could have been there to witness and see how God was using his girls. My father was not only a pastor, but he was a supervisor on his job. One day, while my father was working the building, he caught on fire! Because he had a shepherd's heart, he made sure all the men were out of the building. In doing so, he began to burn inside and out. About the time the fire department and ambulance arrived, my dad had inhaled so much of the smoke and fire that he ended up with four-degree burns. I remember my mother calling us, all eight of us together, along with my aunt, my namesake, to tell us what had happened and that we needed to pray. Before this horrific event, my mom had a dream the night before it happened. We overheard her telling my aunt that God told her to prepare because he was going higher. My father passed. Great sorrow filled our home. We all were able to get through the sorrow with the help of family and friends, and God is with us.

As time went on, so many wonderful things began to happen in the spiritual realm for me. I remember going to the store with my mom. Money was tight after the passing of my father. I wanted something out of the store, and my mom said she did not have any extra money to give me. So, I said, "That's okay, mom, I am going to call Jesus, and He will give me some money." I got out of the car, back then, we had payphones in a booth. I picked up the phone and dialed *Jesus,* and *money* poured out of the phone slot! My mom was amazed, and so were my siblings! I believed! My mother told me later that that act of God was an encouragement to her faith. She said she needed that miracle to happened to carry her through the hard times and sadness of the death of my father.

Another amazing event my mom and I experienced several months after my father passed was one night we were lying in bed, and when I opened my eyes, the room was filled with white doves! When I said, "Mom, look at these beautiful white doves!" She saw them too! When we both said, "Look!" The white doves flew out of the window and the walls, and we heard and felt the window and the walls shake! That was utterly amazing! I will never forget that night! My mother told me after experiencing that, the fear of living in the house was gone, and she was never afraid to be by herself again. God has truly shown Himself great in my life.

Dear reader, I want you to know that if you are afraid or if you are feeling lonely, God can take away your fears and fill your heart with joy. Just trust Him, He is never too busy, God never runs low on His love, and His treasure trove is always on overflow for whatever you need!

"But my God shall supply all your need according to his riches in glory by Christ Jesus" (Philippians 4:19, KJV).

~ Die to Live...~

Deception of the Silent Killer

Deceived

Looking back to that night that my sister and I received the Holy Spirit and were being used mightily by God, things changed. Would you believe even after that indescribable night with the King of Kings and the Lord of Lords and receiving salvation and being filled with the precious Holy Spirit and witnessing all those miracles and events that I still allowed the devil to deceive me and I backslid at the age of eighteen years old! I turned my back on the living God! *Oh*, the *beast*, the BS my flesh was at work like never before with the guidance and help of the evil one! Sometimes even now, I look back on my life and see how crazy and foolish I was to give up God for a season of sin. I truly cannot thank God enough for His *love*, *grace*, and *mercy*!

God gave me another chance. Even in my backslidden state, I was not alone; God was watching over me. I met my boyfriend at the age of twenty-two years old, and one month later, we both would be twenty-three years old. We met in a nightclub of all places. Even in the darkest places in our lives, God is there. God is watching and protecting those who once were in fellowship with Him. He is right there sending soft, gentle text messages to our hearts that He loves us, and He is waiting for us to return back to Him. It does not matter what you have done or what has been done to you, God is waiting for you even now.

God's love is endless…(John 3:16)

~ Die to Live…~

Fate Meets Destiny—The Beast Defeated

Fate in the making. One night my cousin who was living with me said, "Let's go out to the club tonight" I said, "I don't feel like it, but okay." We got dressed, and off we went. The club was standing room only. My cousin and I were sitting at a table, and men were sending drinks over non-stop. I am thankful now that I could not drink. I would have a pina colada or strawberry daiquiri, and my head would feel like it was swimming. So, the drinks would just sit there on the table. Even in the midst of my sinful life, I could hear my mother saying, "If you get a drink and go and dance and the drink is still there when you return, don't drink it because someone could have put something in it." She told me about a story of a beautiful young lady in college that went out with her friends partying, and someone dropped some pills in her drink, and the pills that they gave her damaged her brain. She ended up losing her mind. She did not know who she was, what her name was, she had to be fed and cared for like she was a baby. What a sad real-life story that was, and it has happened to so many boys and girls. That story always would come to my mind when I was out clubbing or partying.

As the night went on, fate walked into the room. It was something about this man that made him stand out. We locked eyes, and he asked me to dance from across the room. I know another guy was at the table trying to talk to me, but It was like I tuned him out, or he was not even there. I just politely got up and walked to this man, and we began to dance. When we started to dance, he just stared at me without blinking his eyes! He would not say a word, he just stared. I asked him, "Are you deaf?" He just stared. He then said, "You are going to marry me," and that he was a preacher! I looked at him like he was crazy! First, I did not know him; secondly, he had got it wrong that I was going to marry him and thirdly, I told him I had never seen a preacher in a nightclub! I thought in my mind there is no way he was a preacher because my father was a preacher, and he never went to a club after he received salvation and began to preach.

This guy was persistent and determined. He would not leave. He stood and watched this other guy beg and beg me for my phone number for over thirty minutes. He did not get involved, he just watched. Finally, the guy gave up and left. Then he walked over and asked me if he could have my number to call me. Normally I would say no, but to this guy, I said yes. "What in the world is going on?" I would ask myself. He was the only guy I called home and told my mother that I met a young man. He was so persistent that he said, "I am going to call you tomorrow at 6 p.m." And sure thing, at 6 p.m. the phone rang on the dot! He had just graduated from college, and he had to let me know. I sat in the middle of the bed with one of those big red thick dictionaries! He used so many big words that I did not know what he was talking about, *lol!*

As time went on, we began to date. Things got serious, and we became an item, or back then, we just said we were boyfriend and girlfriend. Life was good, and the BS, the beast of the flesh, was happy, so we thought until we both were experiencing a tug at our hearts from God. We both tried to ignore it, but we could not. One day he received a phone call from his mother, who had been praying for him. She told him I do not know what you are doing, but God told me He was going to chastise him because he was being disobedient. He knew at the age of nine years old that he was called to preach and pastor, but he did not want that responsibility. He was running from his calling.

God has a way to get your attention. The day he was supposed to go to the Phoenix Suns training camp to try out to play pro basketball, he was hit by an eighteen-wheeler! The discipline had begun! This will begin a life-changing journey. His mother told him God told her that she could not get involved or help him because he was not doing God's will. It was at this time he moved in with me. Conviction of living in sin was eating us up!

During all of this, we were attending church regularly. The Word of God is true. Proverbs 22:6 (EXB): "Train children·to live the right way [in their/*or* his path; referring either to children or to God], and when they are old, they will not stray [depart] from it."

To be honest, we never stop going to church even when we backslid. It was in us to go to church no matter what. We are both thankful that we come from families that told us the truth. We were reminded continuously that living together without being married is a sin, and God was not pleased with it. My boyfriend not only was called to the ministry, but I was also too. While attending church, we were active. My boyfriend was a great musician. We began traveling with our pastor, who was my brother, and his wife everywhere they went.

Our pastor was wise in his approach and the way he council us about our sinful situation. The BS, the beast of our flesh, was happy, but our souls were saddened. We set a time to sit down to have one of the most serious talks we would ever have. This is my opinion: I believe marriage is the second most important decision we can make after salvation because the man and the woman become united as one in every area of their lives. We told each other that neither one of us was worthy of each other going to hell. With a great conviction on us, we had to decide if we should get married. We both agreed that we would pray and ask God if it was His will for us to marry. We slept separately that night because we wanted no interference. The next day came, and we were ready to hear what God had said. I went first, and I told him God told me yes, and he said God told him yes as well. I felt a release in my soul. I was so hungry for God. In our church, we had altar calls, and I went up for prayer every service. I did not care what people had to say because it was just that serious! I wanted to have God the Holy Spirit back in my soul like I did when I was young. One night we were lying in bed, and we both said we wanted to be used by God as the disciples that when they passed by, people were healed just from their shadows! We wanted God urgently. We told our pastor, and he gave us the suggestion to go get our marriage licensed and get married after church and then plan a big reception later. We took his advice, and I only told my mother our plan.

The Day of Reconciliation came as we looked back into the calendar of our soul and seen mercy at its best because we did not die in our sins.

> However, you are not [living] in the flesh [controlled by the sinful nature] but in the Spirit, if in fact the Spirit of God lives in you [directing and guiding you]. But if anyone does not have the Spirit of Christ, he does not belong to Him [and is not a child of God].

> Romans 8:9 (AMP)

Just the thought of living in sin for one year and four months being controlled by the sinful nature and being dry and dead inside and knowing that life was back in our souls we could not sleep that night! The day came, and we got married! I will never forget that Friday night on March 9th that our souls were purified back to God, and we became as one for the first time in our lives. I did not get the fairytale wedding with the white dress but what I did get was the greatest gift that a human being can receive, and that is the gift of the Holy Spirit!

The presence of God showered us with His anointing, and His Holy Spirit filled the sanctuary. There was not a dry eye in the building. The *beast was defeated* in the area of living in sin and un marital sex. We were free! Our souls were free! Free for the Holy Spirit to dwell in us once again. I do believe, according to the Word of God that the Holy Spirit will not dwell in an unclean temple. Our souls were cleansed and available for the Holy Spirit to take full control!

My soul is singing Andre Crouch's songs, "I don't know why Jesus loved me, I don't know why He cared, I don't know why He sacrificed His life, Oh, but I'm glad, so glad He did!"

We completely yielded to God and never turned back! We have been serving God, working in ministry, and married now for over thirty years. To God be the glory!

~ Die to Live... ~

The Beast of Deception

Deception hurts so bad. Have you ever been deceived? How did you feel after the deception? I do not know about you, but I have been deceived so many times in my life. It is not a good feeling or outcome. I felt robbed, taken advantage of. I remember putting my trust in one of my best friends from high school. We were besties! It was three of us that hung out together all the time. We spent the night at each other houses, we shopped together, ate together, we just had fun! If it was not any fun, we made up fun! After graduation, the time we once shared started to diminish due to college and working, etc., the three amigos turned into the two amigos. Our other friend that was a part of us seemed to have disappeared. We found out years later that she got pregnant and did not want anyone to know, so she distanced herself from everyone.

I was about nineteen years old when the deception that changed our friendship happened. My BFF, or should I say I thought she was my best friend, ended up stealing my wallet with all my money in it! I had about eight hundred thousand in cash in it because I was working as a temp during the Christmas holidays at the post office, and during that time, you could work as many overtime hours as you wanted. She knew I had just got paid because we had made plans to go out that night. When I confronted her, she told me it was not her and that she would never do that to me. She was so convincing, and so is the devil. I was crying and extremely upset! I told her, "Whoever took it can have the money, I just needed my wallet because my driver's license and SSN card, etc., was in it, and I had a job interview coming up, and I needed my identification information to get the job."

After I calmed down, I believed her, surely my BFF, my bestie, would not steal from me, but low and behold, the next day, my cousin saw her come back to my mom's house and throw my wallet in the front yard! I was devastated!

I could hear my mother's words in my ear do not trust those girls. They are not your true friends. If I only knew then what I know now that parents that love us really do have our backs! Psalm 118:8 (KJV) says: " **It** is better to trust in the LORD **than to put confidence in man.**"

Don't believe [trust] your neighbor or trust [put confidence in] a friend.

Don't say anything [Guard the doors of your mouth], even to your wife [the one who lies on your bosom].

After that, our friendship was never the same. We slowly drifted apart, and we went our separate ways. Time went on, and I found myself somewhat alone. As I viewed my life, I ask myself did I have any true friends? My eyes were beginning to open to life, and what I saw I did not like. I started back going to church regularly. I was hurting. I was so naïve! The devil loves it when we are naïve and immature. This is a great opportunity for the devil to take advantage of us when we are hurting because we are very vulnerable. The devil prey on our weaknesses. If you are hurting, feeling down and out, we have a Savior Jesus, that is waiting to comfort you right now with His arms opened wide. I pray that you receive His love, comfort, and protection over your heart in Jesus's name.

~ Die to Live… ~

Deception in the Church

This is where the devil crosses enemy lines! He has deceived many who preach and teach the Gospel of Jesus Christ to compromise the Word of God! I am at a loss for words because we know the Bible says in Proverbs 30:5-6 (AMP):

> Every word of God is tested *and* refined [like silver]; He is a shield to those who trust *and* take refuge in Him. Do not add to His words, Or He will reprove you, and you will be found a liar.

Proverbs 30:5-6 (AMP)

Deuteronomy 4:2 (NIV): "Do not add to what I command you and do not subtract from it but keep the commands of the LORD your God that I give you."

Don't simply mean *do not*. God is commanding us not to add or subtract from His Word. The Word of God, the truth, is what is going to make, compel, force, require, and will set us free! The truth of the Word will make you free from sin or whatever entangles you!

I wondered how anyone can have the boldness the audacity to add or subtract, take away, detract, or lesson what Jesus said!

> In the beginning there was the Word [the Word already existed; the Word refers to Christ,

123

God's revelation of himself]. The Word was with
[in the presence of; in intimate relationship with]
God [the Father], and the Word was [fully] God.

John 1:1 (EXB)

Where in this scripture did it say that man was with God in the beginning? Did it not say that the Word already existed, and the Word was Christ? So, what would make a man think that they can re-do, re-write Jesus? God is serious about His Word! Everything will diminish before the Word. Matthew 24:35 (KJV): "Heaven and earth shall pass away, but my words shall not pass away."

The BS the beast the flesh is simply out of control when it thinks God needs their help to change the Word of God or get God's message across!

The Word is our road map to life and heaven. Who is man to try to redirect God's souls on the map of life, taking them on a wild goose chase, detours, and pitfalls? God has given us the best GPS that there will ever be, and that is the Holy Spirit.

All that Jesus has done to redeem us back to the Father, why would man want to take away from the Word of God or make *salvation* a cheap way out! God forbids!

Dictionary.com defines "true" as "real," "genuine," "authentic." We have a responsibility to know the Word of God. John 8:32 (NIV) says, "Then you will know the truth, and the truth will set you free."

The Word is true all by itself, no and (adding) buts (subtracting) about it. We know what our name is, right? And if someone tells you your name is something different, you do not believe them because you *know* what your name is. You do not argue with them, you do not get upset because you know for a fact the truth is your name is John Doe. We must *know* for a *fact* that the Word of God is true, so when someone tries to deceive us by telling us something that isn't in the Word, making up their own words adding and subtracting, we will not receive it nor believe it because we know the truth.

Second Timothy 2:15 (EXB) tells us to make every effort:

Make every effort [Do your best; Be diligent] to give [present] yourself to God as the kind of person he will approve. Be a worker who is not ashamed [*or* will not be shamed] and who uses the true teaching in the right way [correctly handles the true message/word of truth; *or* holds carefully to the true message/word of truth].

2 Timothy 2:15 (EXB)

We must use the true teaching of the Word of God in the right way, no matter if you are not a preacher, teacher, evangelist, pastor, etc. because we are disciples of Jesus Christ. We have to correctly handle the true message, the word of truth because we are teaching our children, families, friends, co-workers, neighbors, our FB, Twitter, YouTube or social media community, etc., whoever we talk to or have their eyes on us we are teaching, leading and guiding in some kind of way. Deception is real, and that is a fact. The devil is the father of deception, and he tries everything he can to deceive mankind.

You are of *your* father the devil, and it is your will to practice the desires [which are characteristic] of your father. He was a murderer from the beginning and does not stand in the truth because there is no truth in him. When he lies, he speaks what is natural to him, for he is a liar and the father of lies *and* half-truths.

John 8:44 (AMP)

Friends, once again, deception hurts, and we do not have to continue being abused by any deceiver. We have the Word of God and the Holy Spirit with us, aiding us in every area of our lives. Let us be attentive and adhere to the voice of the Lord so we will not be deceived by deception.

~ Die to Live...~

Die to Live

Philippians 1:21 (NIV): "For to me to live is Christ, and to die is gain."

This whole book is centered on the crucifixion and the execution of the flesh, the beastly spirit. Dealing with death is difficult; it does not matter if it is physical death or spiritual death, it is hard. It is extremely difficult to say goodbye to our loved ones because we will miss them on this earth. I believe it is even harder to deal with the death of our own self, our will, and our way. Our loved ones are gone, but we must deal with self our flesh on a day-to-day basis. When we accept Jesus Christ as Savior, the process of the crucifixion of the sinful nature of our flesh begins as we are buried in Christ in God. If we want to experience the life that we were created to live, then we must die to self our flesh. We must die to our sinful nature, our sinful wants and desires, and accept the way of life given to us by Jesus Christ. Die to live.

It is only when we live in Christ that we are made alive!

We know that our old life [self; person] died with Christ on the cross so that our sinful selves [or body controlled by sin; body of sin] would have no power over us and we would not be slaves to sin. Anyone who has died is made free [justified; declared righteous] from sin's control [sin]. [Now; But] If we died with Christ, we know [have confidence; believe] we will also live with him. Christ was raised from the dead, and we know that he cannot die again. Death has no power [mastery;

dominion] over him now. Yes [For; Because], when Christ died, he died to defeat the power of sin [to take away sin; *or* with reference to sin] one time—enough for all time [once for all; Hebrews 7:27]. [But] He now has a new life, and his new life is with [*or* for the glory of; *or* with reference to] God. In the same way, you should see [count; consider] yourselves as being dead to the power of sin [sin] and alive with [to; with reference to] God through [*or* in; in union with] Christ Jesus. So, do not let sin control your life [reign; rule over you] here on earth [in your mortal body] so that you do what your sinful self wants to do [obey/submit to its (evil/sinful) desires]. Do not offer the parts of your body [*or* any part of yourself; your parts/ members] to serve sin, as things to be used in doing [instruments/weapons of] evil [un-righteousness; injustice]. Instead, offer yourselves to God as people who have died and now live. Offer the parts of your body [*or* every part of yourself; your parts/members] to God to be used in doing good [as instruments/weapons of righteousness/justice].[For] Sin will not be your master [exercise dominion/power over you], because you are not under law but under God's grace.

Romans 6:6-14 (EXB)

I Die Daily

The flesh is our enemy, and it is determined to have its way! This is a daily fight that we must fight. First Corinthians 15:31 (AMP) says: "I assure you, believers, by the pride which I have in you in [your union with] Christ Jesus our Lord, I die daily [I face death and die to self]."

We want to die daily to the sinful nature. We want to die daily to our will and our way. In this daily fight with the beastly spirit, our flesh will remain as long as we are on this earth.

And He was saying to them all, "If anyone wishes to follow Me [as My disciple], he must deny himself [set aside selfish interests], and take up his cross daily [expressing a willingness to endure whatever may come] and follow Me [believing in Me, conforming to My example in living and, if need be, suffering or perhaps dying because of faith in Me]. For whoever wishes to save his life [in this world] will [eventually] lose it [through death], but whoever loses his life [in this world] for My sake, he is the one who will save it [from the consequences of sin and separation from God]. For what does it profit a man if he gains the whole world [wealth, fame, success], and loses or forfeits himself?

Luke 9:23-25 (AMP)

If we want to follow Jesus and be one of Jesus's disciples, we must deny and refute our *self*ish interests or our selfish concerns and pursuits. Wherever we see *self,* that is the flesh, the beastly spirit, BS. If it were up to us, we would want everything our way. If we were in the Bible days looking at how people are today, I can imagine some people trying to tell Jesus what to do. Arguing back and forward, trying to prove their point. Well, believe it or not, that is what we do when Jesus tell us to do something rather it is in prayer or through his Word, from our pastors, etc. we ignore Him, we give Him the hand and tell Him, "Wait a minute I am not doing that, I already had in mind what I was going to do." This is a prime example of why self, our flesh, needs to die so we will accept the will of God.

Empty without the Holy Spirit

Our souls are without significance, meaningless, and worthless if we do not have Jesus and the filler the Holy Spirit. As the scripture said above, what does it profit a (man) person to gain the whole world's wealth, fame, success, and loses or forfeits himself? Sin is the separator. Sin separates us from God, from the Holy Spirit. We cannot live a life pleasing to God without Jesus, we need him greatly.

Without Christ, we are spiritually dead, empty, and void of the Holy Spirit.

Without the Holy Spirit, we have nothing to change the old nature, the fleshly BS mind into the mind of Christ. We need the Holy Spirit to convict us when we are wrong, when we sin, when we think immoral thoughts, when we think adversely. We need the Holy Spirit to lead, guide, and direct us in the will of God. If we want to please God and do His will, then the flesh must die. I cannot say it enough we must die to live.

I have been crucified with Christ [that is, in Him I have shared His crucifixion]; it is no longer I who live, but Christ lives in me. The *life* I now live in the body I live by faith [by adhering to, relying on, and completely trusting] in the Son of God, who loved me and gave Himself up for me.

Galatians 2:20 (AMP)

Don't Be a Zombie

Once we received Jesus as Savior, there is supposed to be a difference in us. We do not want to be like the walking dead. Walking and talking, going, and doing, working, and partying but dead! A zombie! The beast, our flesh, is the living dead. My husband loves watching scary movies. Zombies are extremely popular now in movies. I see the flesh the BS like a zombie! Zombies do not listen to anyone; they do whatever they want to do. Zombies are dead, just like people who refuse to accept Jesus Christ as Savior are spiritually dead. Zombies feed off other people's brains just like the flesh feeds off what it sees and wants. Zombies have no direction, they just walk around looking and looking, searching, and searching, trying to find something, anything. Have you noticed that dead zombies hang out with other dead zombies? Zombies look different from the living. When you see them, you know right away that they are a zombie. They look dead and act dead because they are dead. There are so many zombies sitting in church. Singing, praying, preaching, ushering, playing instruments, or just sitting on the pews but have not been made alive through Christ Jesus. Just a zombie, lifeless, going through the motions in the house of the Lord, refusing to accept Jesus as Savior.

How sad is that? Jesus is life! Jesus is so wonderful! Jesus *died* so that we could *live*! Why not choose life and live!

Display Jesus

Are you dying to the flesh the beast, that life will be exhibited? Do your life model or display Jesus? Are you dying to live? Are you living in the purpose God created you for? We can live in Christ and not in the purpose that God has created us for, and what we think we are doing is a minus in our lives, not an addition. We all have a meaning to life on this earth. Our enemy, the devil, does not want us to know our purpose in life, so he tries to do whatever he can to confuse us, get us off track, busy us up so we cannot focus. Stay focus and implanted in the Word of God. The Word is our plan to a victorious life here on this earth and eternity.

Colossians 3:1-10 (EXB) is titled Your New Life in Christ—let us read:

[Therefore] Since you were raised from the dead [raised] with Christ, aim at [aspire to; seek after; focus on] what is in heaven [the things above], where Christ is sitting at the right hand of God. Think only about [Set your minds on; Fix your thoughts on] the things in heaven [above], not the things on earth. [For] Your old sinful self has [You] died, and your new life is kept [hidden] with Christ in God. When Christ, who is your life, comes again [appears; is revealed], you will share in his [be revealed with him in] glory. So put all evil [earthly; worldly] things out of your life [to death]: sexual sinning, doing evil [impurity; defilement], letting evil thoughts control you [lust; passion], wanting things that are evil [selfish desires], and greed, which is serving a false god [idolatry]. Because of these things, God's judgment [anger; wrath] is coming. You also used to do these things [live/walk this way] when you were part of the world [living among/in them]. But now also put these things out of your life: anger, bad temper [rage], hatred [malice; evil], saying things to hurt others [slander; blasphemy], and using evil words [abusive/ filthy/obscene language] when you talk [from your mouth]. Do not lie to each other. You have left [taken/tripped off; *or* disarmed;] your old sinful life [self; person; man] and the things you did before [its deeds/practices]. You have begun to live the new life [put on the new person/man], in which you are being made new [renewed] in the true knowledge of God [knowledge] and are becoming like [according to the image of] the One who created you.

Colossians 3:1-10 (EXB)

Jesus called the crowd together with His disciples, and said to them, "If anyone wishes to follow Me [as My disciple], he must deny himself [set aside selfish interests], and take up his cross [expressing a willingness to endure whatever may come] and follow Me [believing in Me, conforming to My example in living and, if need be, suffering or perhaps dying because of faith in Me]. For whoever wishes to save his life [in this world] will [eventually] lose it [through death], but whoever loses his life [in this world] for My sake and the gospel's will save it [from the consequences of sin and separation from God]. For what does it benefit a man to gain the whole world [with all its pleasures], and forfeit his soul? For what will a man give in exchange for his soul *and* eternal life [in God's kingdom]? For whoever is ashamed [here and now] of Me and My words in this adulterous and sinful generation, the Son of Man will also be ashamed of him when He comes in the glory of His Father with the holy angels."

Mark 8:34-38 (AMP)

Friends, this is it; dying to live is the main emphasis of this book. This death the Bible is instructing us to do in Mark's eighth chapter is a good death. We must die to BS our flesh in order to live. The definition of "die" is to become indifferent, to pass out of existence: *cease*.

Jesus died; He paid an inexpressible price for us to become one of His disciples. If we are to follow Christ, we must give up wanting our way, our will, wanting to live in sin. Jesus said we must die to selfish interests and have a willingness to endure life challenges like He would. Jesus is our example of dying to his will and excepting the will of His Father. Just as Jesus suffered and died, so we must suffer and die for our faith. This is all a part of the execution of the flesh. Mark 8:34 from the Expanded version says:

Then Jesus called the crowd to him, along with his followers [disciples]. He said, "If people [anyone wants] want to follow me, they must give up the things they want [deny themselves; set aside their own interests]. They must·be willing even to give up their lives to [take up their cross and] follow me."

Mark 8:34 (EXB)

Nevertheless, it must become a part of our everyday decisions. This is going to be a process; believe me, it is not going to be overnight. The flesh is not going to be willing to just stop doing what it wants to do, so do not get frustrated or upset if you give in to the BS. Take each day one day at a time, just have in your heart and mind that I am not in control. I am the first to say giving up things I want and things that interest me is hard to do, but it can be done.

I experienced this verse first hand:

> Take up his cross [expressing a willingness to endure whatever may come] and follow Me [believing in Me, conforming to My example in living and, if need be, suffering or perhaps dying because of faith in Me].

> (Matthew 16:24, AMP)

Dying to My Flesh, My Way

One day my husband told me the Lord told him to move to Kentucky. I could not believe this! Why would God tell us to quit our jobs, sell our homes, and move to a place that we had no family and friends? Why would God take me from my family? My family is close-knitted. We went to church together, we had family gatherings every week, sometimes every day we were with my family. During that time, no one in my family had ever left Florida. Why did it have to be me? Things were easy, and I loved it! I was living in a secure plush pillow comfort zone life! If I had a need, all I had to do is call my mom, and the need was met. Of course, I wanted my way. When you want something so bad, you will take uncompromising and drastic measures to have your way. I would have people praying for us to stay. I would go up in prayer lines hoping that the evangelist would say stay! My flesh wanted to rule and have its way! One day I quieted my soul and mind and prayed. I asked God if this were His will, and if it were, I would deny myself and accept His will because I love Him, and I wanted to please Him. My flesh was slowly being crucified as I set aside my interests, wants, and desire to follow Jesus.

So, after much prayer and fasting, we packed up our home and follow Jesus to Kentucky and never looked back.

In life, throughout our day, we face different situations where we must deny ourselves to follow Jesus. God is so loving and merciful that He has blessed us with the Holy Spirit. The Holy Spirit is with us at all times to lead and guide us if we allow Him to. I know that is easier said than done because the beast, our flesh, is not giving up. It sounds so easy to say just allow the Holy Spirit to do its job, that would be great if that was all we had to do, but the enemy inside the BS our flesh is right there with its hands up throwing punches fighting against the Holy Spirit.

The BS knows that however old we are, that is how long we have been making our own decisions, and it does not want to stop now. If we want to die to our flesh and live, we must yield to God's way. We have a choice throughout the day, and the bottom line is that no matter what the outcome is, we had to give ourselves the permission to make the choice to live or to die.

How to Stay Dead

> But I say, walk *habitually* in the [Holy] Spirit [seek Him and be responsive to His guidance], and then you will certainly not carry out the desire of the sinful nature [which responds impulsively without regard for God and His precepts]. For the sinful nature has its desire which is opposed to the Spirit, and the [desire of the] Spirit opposes the sinful nature; for these [two, the sinful nature and the Spirit] are in direct opposition to each other [continually in conflict], so that you [as believers] do not [always] do whatever [good things] you want to do.
>
> Galatians 5:16-17 (AMP)

Reading these verses, some of the words that stand out to me to help the flesh to stay dead are habitually (continually), seek, responsive, and guidance.

What does it mean to walk habitually? I believe it means that we are to live continuously, every day, never stopping in the guidance of the Holy Spirit.

We are to pursue and follow the Holy Spirit and be receptive and open to His supervision, leadership, direction and give Him control; then, the BS will certainly not carry out the desire of itself, which is the sinful nature. The sinful nature answers thoughtlessly, uncaringly, and insensitively without any respect for God and His teachings and principles.

This flesh, the BS, has its cravings and wants. The BS is in conflict and in a battle, a war with the Holy Spirit. The sinful nature of our flesh is in direct disagreement and hostile with the Holy Spirit. So, if we want to die to live, then we must adhere to and obey the Word of God

> However, you are not [living] in the flesh [controlled by the sinful nature] but in the Spirit, if in fact the Spirit of God lives in you [directing and guiding you]. But if anyone does not have the Spirit of Christ, he does not belong to Him [and is not a child of God].

Romans 8:9 (AMP)

If we want to receive all the benefits that Jesus offers, we must have the Holy Spirit. I cannot emphasize enough that we must have the Holy Spirit. The Holy Spirit is the power of God. The Holy Spirit is available to anyone who repents and surrenders their life to God. Isn't that wonderful that we do not have to work for it! It is a gift! The Holy Spirit is a gift that never breaks, or needs a battery, a gift that cannot be bought in a store because it was bought with the blood of Jesus Christ, wrapped in His power, and packed in the anointing of God, and specially delivered to the believer! Oh, sweet wonder! I feel the Presence of God just writing about it! It is available right now. Receive it and soar into greater!

~ *Die to Live...* ~

Let the Holy Spirit Be Your Scale

I believe for us to have a balanced life, we must ask the Holy Spirit to be our scale. Unfortunately, the BS will always side with the flesh leaving the Holy Spirit with a little. I once was watching a TV show with my son, and it was only PG-13, but it had so much drama and profanity in it that I told him I had enough. He said, "Mom, we have to have a balance," and I said, "Yes, that is true," but my soul has had enough. I literally could not take anymore! The show was wearing me out! All the drama, fighting, and subliminal messages just wore me out, and I think the show is only thirty to forty-five minutes long. I want the Holy Spirit to be my scale and keep me balanced on the balance beam of life! I think this is what happens a lot of times the BS keeps wanting more and more, and we give in to what it wants, and after taking in so much of the things of the world, we become carnal.

I see balance as a weapon that the beastly spirit uses against us. I hear this so much in the church world that we need to have balance, well who scale are you using to determine the balance? We need God's scale. We need God's Spirit like never before in every area of our lives. Why is it that the BS most of the time gets the most of us? The BS gets the most of our time! We work eight hours or more, run here and there with the need and wants of our kids, then we are involved in other activities, etc., and when it's God's time, God gets the leftovers, and sadly to say for so many that is nothing. Do not let the BS win! Stop giving the BS its own way! You have the power within you to do all things through Christ! Set your gage to the side of victory because you got this!

For if you are living according to the [impuls-
es of the] flesh, you are going to die. But if [you
are living] by the [power of the Holy] Spirit you
are habitually putting to death the sinful deeds
of the body, you will [really] live forever.

Romans 8:13 (AMP)

~ Die to Live...~

We Are the Representatives of Jesus

Do not let unwholesome [foul, profane, worthless, vulgar] words ever come out of your mouth, but only such *speech* as is good for building up others, according to the need *and* the occasion, so that it will be a blessing to those who hear [you speak]. And do not grieve the Holy Spirit of God [but seek to please Him], by whom you were sealed *and* marked [branded as God's own] for the day of redemption [the final deliverance from the consequences of sin]. Let all bitterness and wrath and anger and clamor [perpetual animosity, resentment, strife, fault-finding] and slander be put away from you, along with every kind of malice [all spitefulness, verbal abuse, malevolence]. Be kind *and* helpful to one another, tender-hearted [compassionate, understanding], forgiving one another [readily and freely], just as God in Christ also forgave you.

Ephesians 4:29-32 (AMP)

The Carnality of the BS

Carnality means living a life consumed by satisfying fleshly desires, feeding selfishness while serving the body, and starving the soul. Carnality is the state of depravity. Depravity—immorality, decadence, evil, wickedness, corruption (Dictionary.com).

The carnal carnality of the flesh the beast has crept into the Body of Christ to the point that the church world has come accustomed to it and thinks that it is okay. The devil wants us to stay carnal. The devil loves it when we do not take on or live a holy and separated life as Jesus did. There are so many areas in our lives that we take off the clothes of righteousness and put on the outfit of carnality. Can you imagine if we changed clothes every time, we switched out from holy to unholy we would wear ourselves out! Well, we should feel tired living like turning a light switch on and off all day. One minute I am living for Jesus, the next minute I am back into the flesh, the BS. One area we see the switch going on and off is with words, we hear small curse words "shit," "damn," "hell no," "ass," etc., and some even go as far as to say the f-word! These words are offensive even when someone says, "Excuse me for saying that." How many excuses will it take to know that Jesus never had slippers?

Can you imagine Jesus talking like this? Saying words like we hear people that say they are saved saying? I cannot! This is one of the reasons why we need the Holy Spirit like never before. The devil wants us to think it is okay to do small things because he knows smalls things can cause big results! It is not okay no matter what when the BS the beastly spirit tells us to act unseemly and have a polluted mouth. We are the *representatives of Jesus Christ*! We have been elected by God to appear as Jesus, act like Jesus, and speak for Jesus. We are supposed to build one another up with our words. Our words should be intended to be a blessing. Do we think the devil wants us to represent Jesus as He is? No! He wants us to act like the world, talks like the world, and, most of all, sin as the world. The devil knows sin causes death. No matter how small or large the sin is, death will follow.

~ Die to Live…~

Grieve not the Holy Spirit

Grieve—mourn, pain, sadden, upset

As representatives of Jesus, we must follow the leading of the Holy Spirit. There are so many ways to grieve and upset the Holy Spirit. The Scripture told us to get rid of all bitterness and wrath, and anger and clamor perpetual animosity, resentment, strife, fault-finding, and slander should be put away from us, along with every kind of malice, all spitefulness, verbal abuse, malevolence. If we choose to side with our flesh and be bitter and have wrath, anger, resentment, strife, and the list goes on, we will grieve the Holy Spirit. We grieve the Holy Spirit when we allow the BS to be in control of our actions and words.

We grieve the Holy Spirit when we sin, use abusive, vulgar, and profane language. It is of the utmost importance that we as Christians live, walk, and talk in a way that is representing Jesus. Overriding the Holy Spirit doing our own will and way grieves the Spirit. Refusing to acknowledge the Holy Spirit grieves Him. Refusing to be obedient to the Word of God grieves the Holy Spirit. When we do not *love* everyone with a pure heart, grieve the Holy Spirit. The Holy Spirit is the Spirit of God living inside of the Body of Christ aiding us to be the representative of Jesus that we should be. Let us be the light the representatives for Jesus in a world that is dark and sick with sin and hatred.

If we want to please God in our daily lives, then we must not grieve and sadden the Holy Spirit. Do not reject but accept the Holy Spirit, for we are the representatives of our Savior Jesus Christ.

~ Die to Live… ~

Imbued by the Holy Spirit

~ Personal Trainer ~

My soul is leaping! I was on a conference prayer, and one of our deacons talked about the mind. He said he saw an interview with Stephen Curry, who is the greatest shooter in basketball in the *world*! They asked him how he became to be so great, did he practice shooting all the time? He said, "No, I have trained my mind, and my body has followed!" My God! That did it for me! The Holy Spirit set off a bomb inside my soul! That was on a Sunday, on the next day, I went into a consecration, denying myself of all food until 6 p.m. for the rest of the week. I ask God to allow the Holy Spirit to train my mind! I wanted the Holy Spirit to be my personal trainer in every area of my life!

I prayed, asking the Holy Spirit to train me how and when to pray. Train me the Word of God, train me how to love like Jesus, train me how to preach and teach and evangelize the Word of God, train me how to love like Jesus, act like Jesus, talk and walk like Jesus! Train me to be effective in everything for His glory. Train me to be the best wife, mother, friend, sister, aunt, etc., train me to write books like never before in Jesus's name! Train me how to use the gifts and talents You have given me. Train me how to sing and lead Your people into praise and worship. Train my mouth to speak life and liberty! Excitement had taken me over! I had to respond to this excitement and eagerness before it left me. Since I have never had a personal trainer, I had to do some research. I found out that a personal trainer has the ability to change lives for the better.

A personal trainer helps clients achieve their fitness and health goals through motivation and education. Being a personal trainer is much more than giving out exercise orders. I thought about it if a human being can help change lives for the better for people, then surely the Holy Spirit as a Trainer can transform a person's mind, body, and soul permanently. I don't know what it is like to have a personal trainer, but I do know some people who have had a PT, and they experienced weight loss, but soon after they were no longer in the PT care, the weight came back on.

I believe if the Holy Spirit trains us, then we can be assured that He will never leave us and the changes that take place is lasting. How wonderful it is spiritually that we do not have to worry about getting older and having sagging muscles. In the spiritual realm, it is the opposite of the world's view of getting older. In the spiritual realm, the older you get after training years and years with the Holy Spirit, your spiritual muscles get bigger and stronger as time goes on, soon you will be the incredible hulk spiritually and can handle the weights of life with ease and confidence!

I found out that a personal trainer guides their clients step by step throughout their whole routine, whether it is in a gym or boot camp. They are passionate about health and fitness, and through their work, inspire and encourage others to develop healthy habits and routines through the safe delivery of effective programs, instruction, motivation, and education.

Oh, this is good! Are you thinking spiritually what I am thinking? The Bible tells us that the Holy Spirit is our

> But the Helper (Comforter, Advocate, Intercessor—Counselor, Strengthener, Standby), the Holy Spirit, whom the Father will send in My name [in My place, to represent Me and act on My behalf], He will teach you all things. And He will help you remember everything that I

have told you.

John 14:26 (AMP).

I believe no matter how young you are in the boot camp of your salvation, the Holy Spirit will be there with you, and if you are a general or a captain in your salvation journey, the Holy Spirit is right there for you as well in the gym of life. Who is more concerned about your total being than God? Our Father wants us to be healthy and fit spiritually and naturally. There is no greater encourager and motivator than the Holy Spirit!

The Gym of Life

The first thing people do to become fit is to change their eating habits. Spiritually for us to be fit for the kingdom, we have to change or add to our eating habits. Looking through the spiritual lenses in the gym of life, I visualize the muscles (strength) as the *Word of God*. In the natural, if we have weak muscles in our body, we will feel fatigued, exhausted. In the spiritual, if we do not eat the Word of God, we will become weak and frail, and delicate. Have you ever met a delicate Christian? They are easy to be offended, they wear their feeling on their sleeves. Often there is a negative spirit attached due to weakness and frailty. They are always looking for a fault in something or somebody. You feel like you must tiptoe through the tulips when you are around them. What an uncomfortable feeling! Let us face it, we need the Word of God daily to stay strong!

If we want to grow up and mature as we eat the Word. The

Word is free! The Word never gets stale or old! There is no expiration date; it is good until eternity. We can eat the word at any time of the day or night and always get the best nutrients for our souls. The word is food that we are encouraged to eat as much as we want, snack as much as we want until we are stuffed!

We must eat daily. If we do not eat the Word of God, we will stay in baby-Christian status longer. How can a baby defend itself? It cannot. The enemy loves it when we do not grow spiritually. But if we eat the healthy Word of God daily or three times or more a day as we do with food, not only will we grow stronger in our walk, stronger in our faith, and we begin to feel better.

We would begin to lay aside and lose the weights and the sins that so easily entangles us. The BS, the beast of the flesh, will be stripped off because the truth of the Word will bring conviction and clarity to the way we ought to live and causing us to be set free.

Hebrews 12:1-3 lets us know that we are in a race. We are athletes that are training for the greatest metal of victory that could ever be given to mankind, and that is the crown of eternal life!

> Therefore, since we are surrounded by so great a cloud of witnesses [who by faith have testified to the truth of God's absolute faithfulness], stripping off every unnecessary weight and the sin which so easily *and* cleverly entangles us, let us run with endurance *and* active persistence the race that is set before us, [looking away from all that will distract us and] focusing our eyes on Jesus, who is the Author and Perfecter of faith [the first incentive for our belief and the One who brings our faith to maturity], who for the joy [of accomplishing the goal] set before Him endured

the cross, disregarding the shame, and sat down at the right hand of the throne of God [revealing His deity, His authority, and the completion of His work]. Just consider *and* meditate on Him who endured from sinners such bitter hostility against Himself [consider it all in comparison with your trials], so that you will not grow weary and lose heart.

Hebrews 12:1-3 (AMP)

Praise God for the victory! Hallelujah!

Strength ~ Prayer

Now that we are working our muscles, we need strength. I envision strength as *prayer*. Little prayer—little strength; much prayer—much strength! My mother would always tell me that prayer is the only way to talk to God. We need the strength of God to continue in this race. Prayer helps us to strip off every unnecessary weight and the sin which so easily and cleverly entangles us. Prayer helps us to run with endurance and active persistence in the race that is set before us. Prayer helps us to look away from all that will distract us and focus our eyes on Jesus, who is the author and perfecter of the faith. Prayer will help us to bring our faith to maturity. We must have the strength to endure all that life will bring.

First Thessalonians 5:17 (NLT): "Never stop praying."

Tone Your Body

You may hear when exercising that we need to tone your body. The dictionary definition of tone is our character, attitude, mood, spirit, flavor, temper, humor, tenor, vein, disposition, and essence.

Let us probe into some of the words defined from *tone*. The first one is character; our character is what defines who we are. Jesus's character is compassionate, loving, serving, forgiving, committed, prayerful, gentle, patient, self-control, humble. The beast in us does not want us to have the tone of Jesus, it wants its own tone. What is your tone? How do people see you? The greater question is, "How does God see you?"

I believe if the Body of Christ showed more love, compassion, empathy, kindness to one another and non-believers, we would win more souls to Christ!

Jesus exhibited His love by dying on the cross for all the sins of the world. Then giving us an overflow of love by sending back the Holy Spirit. There are so many examples of Jesus's tone in the Word. Just looking at the woman with the issue of blood, what great compassion Jesus has shown by stopping and acknowledging that someone had touched Him.

Have you ever thought about what kind of mood was Jesus in? We can be certain that His mood, His disposition were not foul or evil. His temperance had to be intact in place to respond and deal with every kind of situation and people. Just imagine if Jesus was hot-headed! We know that we cannot make the best decisions when we are heated and frenzied. What a mess this world would be in if Jesus's tone were like ours. As soon as someone upset Him, He could have had his Angels wipe them out right then and there!

Appearance ~ Attitude

Have you ever heard this saying, "You got an attitude?" The times we are living in, we see so much attitude or another word for it is *drama* from the youngest child to grandparents. We even see drama in the church. We see a great showing of a fleshly spectacle right before our eyes. We can see a vivid performance in the church of the fleshly Beast on every level from the pulpit to the back door. The attitude of the beast is drama! Wanting to be seen. Self is on display, and Christ has been hidden.

There are boldness and an arrogant egotism spirit that we see now more than ever. We see the attitude of pride, self-importance, and conceit that we do not need God or a Pastor to help us or tell us what to do.

The saying now is, "I'm doing me." Do you and get your results! We see the BS of self everywhere from children not wanting to be governed by the parents, leaders don't want to be governed by the pastor, employees want a job with work picked out from it and have an attitude if you correct them. They have the nerves to say, "You don't tell me what to do because I am grown!"

The Beast is out of control! I once had an employee that told me she did not care what the police or a judge would say because they are just a person like she is. So why should it matter what they have to say? Here we can see the BS of no respect for authority.

What kind of attitude, mindset did our Savior Jesus Christ have? Jesus demonstrated an attitude of humility and selflessness. Jesus always had someone or something else on His mind rather than Himself. I cannot imagine Jesus with a negative mind which causes a negative attitude. Jesus's stance was, "I am here on this earth *only* to do the *will* of my *Father.*" He came to fulfill the purpose of bringing *life* back to humanity. He had no other agenda. One purpose, one goal, one aim, one quest, one mission to defeat death once and for all, and He did it by dying for all the sins of the world and raising with all power in His hands! Hallelujah!

Idiosyncratic

Bodybuilders train day after day not only to be fit but some train to win the gold medal in Bodybuilding fitness! Have you ever seen one of the winners? They are idiosyncratic, distinctive, and peculiar! No matter where they go, they are going to stand out. People are going to stare and watch them because they do not look like everybody else. This is how we should look spiritually! First Peter 2:9 (KJV) says: "But ye are a chosen generation, a royal priesthood, an holy nation, a peculiar people; that ye should shew forth the praises of him who hath called you out of darkness into his marvelous light."

The bodybuilder is oiled down. We should be oiled down in the anointing of God; their bodies look like gold brass! If we stay in the fire of our trials and tribulations, we will come out like pure gold. Have you noticed that when they flex their muscles, it gives the body another posture or look? If we flex, stretch our hearts, we can love more, have more compassion and forgiveness toward others, and we will look different too! The bodybuilders are fit and trim! They do not eat junk! They do not hang out with people that are not on the path they are on because they cannot afford to get sidetracked! They do not want to gain any weight, so they eat healthily. Are we eating

Evelyn A. Johnson

healthy from the table of the Word of God?

No matter what, the bodybuilders are determined to win at any cost necessary!

I pose a question, "Are we?" Are we willing to do whatever it takes to please God? Are we willing to humble ourselves and accept the purpose God created us for and do it? Are we willing to do whatever it takes, or whenever it might take us no matter what time of day so we can shine like stars for Christ?

If so, pray this small prayer with me: "Father, we need your help. Help us to be so determined to live a life to please you so when we are being watched, and viewed people will stare and see Jesus the light of glory all over and in us in Jesus Name! Amen."

Energy—Holy Spirit

To train, we need energy. We need energy to do everything! Spiritually the Holy Spirit is our energy! Our vigor, liveliness, get-up-go, oomph, and our dynamism!

~ Accept the Great Helper ~

God has given us help. John 14:16 (AMP) says: "And I will ask the Father, and He will give you another Helper (Comforter, Advocate, Intercessor—Counselor, Strengthener, Standby), to be with you forever..."

If we want the BS to die in every area of our lives, including losing weight and live a life of victory, etc., we have the greatest helper, the Holy Spirit. The Holy Spirit will counsel us and tell us don't do this or that or don't eat that etc., even if we mess up, He will tell us to get back up and try it again. You can make it! The Holy Spirit will give us the strength we need to win. He is right there all the time, waiting to help and assist us. The choice is ours to accept the help or ignore it.

The Holy Spirit will give us the energy to keep fighting the good fight of faith, the getup and go to read the Word, the vigor to love the unlovable, and the dynamism to say no to sin and things that weigh us down.

The Holy Spirit is our *strength*. We need the strength of God to face the everyday life experience. We need the strength of the Holy Spirit to carry the loads of life and all its challenges. Bottle line we need, the Power of God in every area of our lives. Let us power up! Get powered up! Stay powered up!

I am so thankful for the Holy Spirit. I want to be filled and flooded and jam-packed with God's Power! I never will forget a message that our Pastor preached about being filled with the Holy Spirit. He gave an illustration using a water bottle. On the table, he had two water bottles. One was halfway full, and the other was filled to the top. He took the half-filled bottle and poured some soda in it, and the water changed and turned another color, no longer looking like "pure" water. Then he took the bottle that was filled to the top and said, "See how this is filled to the top? I can't pour anything in it because there is no space." He explained that if we are not full of the Holy Spirit that our vessel, our soul has space for contamination to come in.

I think of contamination as an infection. Once the infection gets into our bodies, it causes sickness. Sickness weakens the body, and spiritually when we are sick and weak, it is easy for the devil to defeat us; this is the devil's goal to crush us. He cannot triumph over us if we are filled with the power of God the Holy Spirit.

John 16:7 (KJV): "Nevertheless I tell you the truth; It is expedient for you that I go away: for if I go not away, the Comforter will not come unto you; but if I depart, I will send him unto you."

Jesus knew we would need help from Him to make it on this earth. Jesus knew that the enemy would come against us because he hates Jesus. Jesus said, "I must go!" It is advantageous for you that I do not stay on this earth but go back to heaven and send back the Holy Spirit as a representative of Me. God has made all provisions for His children to be successful while on this journey of life. What a wonderful Father He is that all our needs are met through Him.

> However, you are not [living] in the flesh [controlled by the sinful nature] but in the Spirit, if in fact the Spirit of God lives in you [directing and guiding you]. But if anyone does not have the Spirit of Christ, he does not belong to Him [and is not a child of God].
>
> Romans 8:9 (AMP)

This scripture opens up a can of worms for so many discussions about the Holy Spirit. Just reading it lets us know that we should not be living in our flesh the BS (beastly spirit) or controlled by the sinful nature, but we should be living by the Holy Spirit. I imagine being filled with the Holy Spirit is being like superman! Superman could do incredible things when he was not Clark Kent. When Superman is Clark, he is like everybody else, weak in the flesh in his humanness. When we do not have the Holy Spirit, we are just like any other human being weak in our flesh. Superman, with all his power, could be weakened by one thing, and that was kryptonite. Kryptonite could weaken him draining him of his powers, and overlong exposure to the substance could kill him. For the Christians, our kryptonite is sin! Sin will do the same to us, it will weaken us drain us of the Holy Spirit's which is our power, and overlong exposure to sin will kill us. For the wages of sin is death.

It is when we are empowered by the Holy Spirit, we can do all things through Christ because of His power!

Fill and Flood Me with God Himself

> And [that you may come] to know [practically, through personal experience] the love of Christ which far surpasses [mere] knowledge [without experience], that you may be filled up [throughout your being] to all the fullness of God [so that you may have the richest experience of God's presence in your lives, completely filled and flooded with God Himself].

> Ephesians 3:19 (AMP)

There is a rhetorical question that is if a person living in continuous sin if they are saved? None of us is the judge, only God. We are thankful that the Word of God teaches us, directs us, and guides us. The Bible is clear about sin and what will keep us out of heaven. Nevertheless, if anyone does not have the Holy Spirit, they are not a child of God.

However, you are not [living] in the flesh
[controlled by the sinful nature] but in the Spirit,
if in fact the Spirit of God lives in you [directing
and guiding you]. But if anyone does not have
the Spirit of Christ, he does not belong to Him
[and is not a child of God].

Romans 8:9 (AMP)

I ask God every day to fill me, flood my soul with His Holy Spirit. The Holy Spirit will bring conviction on you as soon as you sin! You will hear lights and sirens going off in your soul! Emergency! Emergency! There is an emergency, get to the emergency room of repentance 911! The Great Physician Jesus is there waiting to forgive you, heal you, and restore you! Do not wait! You might bleed to death! Do not wait, you might stop breathing and die! Sin can bleed and suck the life right out of us! Just like in the natural, if you were bleeding to death or could not breathe, you would get to the hospital. In the spiritual realm, we must do the same thing, get to the hospital of life, and see Jesus! He is never too busy or with another patient. Jesus will wait for you. Thank you, Jesus!

Running on Empty

I can tell when I am running low on the Holy Spirit. Back in the day in our church, we had Friday night service, and the church mothers would say, "Come to the filling station, and get filled back up." We all know that you just cannot drive a car and never put gas in it. We can see the gas stations and keep passing by, and sooner or later, the car will give out of gas, go on empty and stop! That goes for us as well; if we do not get filled back up, we will go on empty and stop! We can find ourselves little by little stopping the things we use to do for God. Little by little, our attendance slacks off, and before we know it, we have to stop coming to church, stop reading the Word, stop praying, stop fasting, stop praising and worshipping God, and the list goes on. At this point, the beast is in full control.

We know there are gas stations just about on every corner, and yet you see people pulled off to the side of the road with a gas can pouring gas into their car because the car ran out of gas, and now it is empty. We know the locations of the gas stations in our city as well as where the churches are located. People see them but keep right on-going day by day, knowing the gage is indicating low fuel. One thing for certain the gas station is not going to throw a rope out at you as you pass by and drag you in, you must choose to drive to the station and fill up. The Holy Spirit is not going to force you to accept Him, you must make the choice. You can be sure of this the Holy Spirit will never be out of power (gas)!

Let us go to the power station of the Holy Spirit daily to stay on full so that when the vicissitudes of life drain us, we will have the power to keep going on.

Healthy Eating

Why are the sweetest, most delicious foods, desserts, and junk food are the most unhealthy and cause the quickest weight gain? The BS says, "*Oh*, but it tastes so good all those chocolates, cakes, pies, cookies, pizza, hamburgers, fries, hotdogs, chips, and ice cream, etc.!" In the natural, junk food causes the most physical problems to the body because of the sugar.

In the spiritual, if we eat junk food, our spiritual being will be unhealthy. The flesh does not want to eat the word when it is correcting us. The flesh wants to hear happy messages! We want sugar! But is that spiritually healthy for us to eat sugar and sweets all the time and no vegetables? How can we build our spiritual mussels on sugar? We need our vegetables. We need all the vitamins that come from the vitamins in vegetables to be healthy. Vegetables may not taste good, but it is good for you! The devil knows he can defeat us when we are weak. The devil wants us weak as sugar water!

Our personal trainer, the Holy Spirit, is standing by in our minds telling us to eat the whole word. Eat and swallow, digest, and absorb the Word of God and let it get in you to break down all the sugar the BS (flesh). Whatever you do not spit it out! Do not spit out the parts of the Word of God that we do not like or offends the BS. Have you heard the saying, "Truth offends?" Well, it does! No one likes being corrected, not even children. We need truth (vegetables). We need our vegetables. Eat them, and do not spit them out. If we spit them out, they are of no benefit to us! We will not get any of the nutrients that are in them to make us healthy. It is almost a waste to have even eaten them if we do not digest them. If we want the beastly spirit to be defeated, we must continue to eat from the spiritual healthy table of God. It is when we are empowered by the Holy Spirit, we can do all things through Christ because of His power, the Holy Spirit.

The gym of life is always open for enrollment. You do not have to pay for the membership because Jesus has paid the membership with His death and sign it with His blood. Enroll today and get fit for eternity!

~ *Die to Live* ~

Defeat the Beast Spirit

Get Dressed

"Put on God's complete set of armor provided for us, so that you will be protected as you fight against the evil strategies of the accuser" (Ephesians 6:11 TPT).

The armor of God is our supernatural wardrobe, the designer is God.

> For our struggle is not against flesh and blood [contending only with physical opponents], but against the rulers, against the powers, against the world forces of this [present] darkness, against the spiritual forces of wickedness in the heavenly (supernatural) places. Therefore, put on the complete armor of God, so that you will be able to [successfully] resist and stand your ground in the evil day [of danger], and having done everything [that the crisis demands], to stand firm [in your place, fully prepared, immovable, victorious]. So stand firm and hold your ground, having tightened the wide band of truth (personal integrity, moral courage) around your waist and having put on the breastplate of righteousness (an upright heart), and having strapped on your feet the gospel of peace in preparation [to face the enemy with firm-footed stability and the readiness produced by the good news]. Above all, lift up the [protective] shield of faith with which you can extinguish all the flaming arrows of the evil one. And take the helmet of salvation, and the sword of the Spirit, which is the Word of God.

> With all prayer and petition pray [with specific
> requests] at all times [on every occasion and in
> every season] in the Spirit, and with this in view,
> stay alert with all perseverance and petition [in-
> terceding in prayer] for all God's people.

Ephesians 6:12-18 (AMP)

Dear reader, we are at war! We are in constant conflict and combat with ourselves. This is a tug of war of life of which one is going to rule. Will it be me or God? This daily fight is the strongest battle we will fight! It is ongoing, nonstop, and can only be won by the *indispensable* weapons of God. In Ephesians, the sixth chapter, Apostle Paul gives us a detailed plan on what we are fighting against and how to win.

Let us probe into the Word and put on the supernatural clothing designed by God.

In conclusion, be strong in the Lord, draw your strength from Him, and be empowered through your union with Him and in the power of His boundless might.

In this fight, we must be strong, robust only in the Lord. The beast of the flesh is extraordinarily strong! We cannot allow our flesh to tell us to draw strength from family or friends or any other entity and not God. We need to be resilient solid, and firm in the Lord and in His power. God's power is infinite, vast, and immeasurable! There is nothing stronger or mightier than God. Therefore, we must stay in alliance with God to be empowered.

Have you ever wondered how important and special we must be to God why the devil just will not let up? The devil is dammed to hell forever, and he wants to take as many souls with him. He must be very jealous of human beings. Lucifer was the most beautiful angel leading everyone in praise. He got exalted and thought he was greater than God! He wanted to be God! He wanted the praise! Now that same spirit is on the earth where humans are exalted thinking that they do not need God, this is madness! The beast of the flesh wants the praise for itself! Humility has vanished, and self is out of control. We must always stay on guard because we are in the fight for our life!

When you take heed to Ephesians 6:10, Paul is wanting us, if nothing else, to get this. Finally, lastly to finish your path and purpose in life, be strong in *God*. Whenever you need strength, draw it from God, it is only through the unification in God will He empower you with His unlimited might!

Always Stay Dressed

What a horrific thought to be in a war with no weapons!

Put on the supernatural clothing that is invisible to the natural, but to the supernatural, it is a mighty force. In war, soldiers never leave their post until the war is over! The Word says: "This is for keeps, a life-or-death fight to the finish against the devil and all his angels."

Every day we dressed either to leave the house for work or go out to do something. Even if we stay in the house, we get dressed. We put on something. We do not walk around nude. Spiritually we should do the same thing. We should get dressed every day in the armor of God. We must stay dressed even when we sleep because the devil tries to attack us in our dreams. He will send a dream just like a horror movie playing in your mind trying to paralyze and benumb your faith. Stay dressed! Let us realize that we cannot defeat the devil in our own strength. We need all the weaponry of God to win!

Put It On, Leave It On

The Bible says to put on; that means we must do something. We must set up a defense against the enemy. His objective is to steal everything we have, from our peace to our penny! He wants to kill our faith, hope, and trust in God. He wants to assassinate our dreams, our goals, and the very purpose we were created for. That is not all He wants to obliterate, eliminate, demolish, and destroy us until there is no trace of us! We cannot afford to give him any latitude, none whatsoever! Get dressed! Stay dressed no matter what, do not take off any of your armor!

The Armor of God

Paul teaches us about six pieces of God's armor that we need. This is not something that you can say you want; we must have the armor of God. We need all the pieces to make up the whole armor. Ironically, it is six pieces? Six is the number of mankind. God knew mankind would need the armor to live on this earth.

The Armor of God: "Belt of Truth, Breastplate of Righteousness, Shield of Faith, Helmet of Salvation, Shoes of the Gospel of Peace, and the Sword of the Spirit."

Now let us explore each piece of the Armor of God so we

can defeat the beast within.

Helmet of Salvation

Put on the full armor of God [for His pre-cepts are like the splendid armor of a heavi-ly-armed soldier], so that you may be able to [successfully] stand up against all the schemes *and* the strategies *and* the deceits of the devil.

Ephesians 6:11 (AMP)

I am starting with the Helmet of Salvation because with-out salvation, we can not wear the Armor of God.

A helmet is a covering. We need the covering of salvation that only comes from accepting Jesus as Savior. Without sal-vation, we are unprotected, defenseless, and vulnerable. Sal-vation unites us back to the Father the Creator. Salvation is what allows us to be able to wear the armor of God. We are God's children, we are a part of the royal priesthood, heirs of God, and joint-heirs with Christ. Salvation brings us in right standing with the Father.

What would we need the armor of God for if we are not in a fight? We fight against spiritual evilness and the devil, but the war is against God and the devil. The devil has been mad at God ever since he was kicked out of heaven! "Jesus said, 'I saw Satan fall like lightning from heaven'" (Luke 10:18, EXB).

The devil is so mad at human beings because we get to live with God and Jesus, and he does not. So, what he tries to do is take anyone that will go with him to hell. Think about it, why would he want us to live in heaven. Imagine what heaven looks like from

> The city was built in a square [lies foursquare], and its length was equal to its width. The angel measured the city with the rod. The city was 1,500 miles long, 1,500 miles wide, and 1,500 miles high [1,200 stadia—its length and width and height are equal; the unit of measure called a stadium was approximately 600 feet]. The angel also measured the wall. It was 216 feet [144 cubits] high [*or* thick; the Greek is ambiguous], by human measurements, which the angel was using. The wall was made of jasper, and the city was made of pure gold, as pure as glass. The foundation stones of the city walls were decorated [ornamented] with every kind of jewel [precious stone; Exodus 28:15–21; Is. 54:11–12]. The first foundation was jasper, the second was sapphire, the third was chalcedony [agate], the fourth was emerald, the fifth was onyx [sardonyx], the sixth was carnelian, the seventh was chrysolite [yellow quartz], the eighth was beryl, the ninth was topaz, the tenth was chrysoprase [turquoise], the eleventh was jacinth, and the twelfth was amethyst [the specific identity of some of these jewels is uncertain]. The twelve gates were twelve pearls, each gate having been made from a single pearl. And the street [main street; square] of the city was made of pure gold as clear as glass. I did not see a temple in the city, because the Lord God Almighty [All-powerful] and the Lamb are the city's temple [a temple representing the presence

of God is not needed because God's presence is throughout the city]. The city does not need the sun or the moon to shine on it, because the glory of God ·is its [gives it] light, and the Lamb is the city's lamp [Isaiah 60:19]. By its light the people of the world [nations] will walk, and the kings of the earth will bring their glory into it [Isaiah 60:1–3]. The city's gates will never be shut on any day [Isaiah 60:11], because there is no night there. The glory and the honor of the nations will be brought into it [as gifts to God]. Nothing unclean [impure; profane; common] and no one who does shameful [detestable; abominable] things or tells lies will ever go into it. Only those whose names are written in the Lamb's book [scroll] of life [3:5] will enter the city.

Revelation 21:16-27 (EXB)

How amazing! Heaven is going to be phenomenal, and this is not all that heaven has to offer! What on earth or in hell is worth losing out on going to heaven! Nothing! Thank you, Jesus, for paying the price for humanity to have salvation.

Now, do you see why the devil does not want us to go to heaven? The devil will fight us tooth and nail every day, trying to get us to give in to his schemes and tricks, trying to make us turn back on God and serve him! Whatever you do, do not fall for his deception. One thing I know from experience is that the devil does not fight against those that are in his army. When I was living in sin, the devil wasn't saying to me, "*Oh* please don't lie," or "Don't have sex out of wedlock," or "*Oh* please go to church," "Please read the Bible," "Forgive, I love it when you forgive," "Please don't kill," "Please don't hate," "Whatever you do love everyone." *Oh no!* I never heard him utter anything to this sort. On the contrary, it was the opposite. When you are out in sin, the devil is not the one tugging at your heart trying to get you to come back to God, that is the Holy Spirit. The devil will make sin appear and seem like it is the best thing ever! He will not tell you there is a price for it.

> And what was the result of [benefit/fruit did you reap from] doing those things that now make you ashamed? [For] Those things only bring [The end/result of those things is] death. But now you are free from sin and have become slaves of God. This brings you [reaps the benefit/fruit of] a life that is only for God [holiness; sanctification], and this gives you life forever [the end/result is eternal life]. [For; Because] The payment [wages] for sin is death. But God gives us the free gift of life forever [eternal life] in Christ Jesus our Lord.

Romans 6: 21-23 (EXB)

Do not let the devil rob you of the riches in glory that God has prepared just for you!

We Are on the Same Team

In the United States, ARM Services would not be preposterous and absurd if we were at war and we begin to fight and kill each other. What would be the need for the enemy to fight against us if we are going to do it for them? I once was told that Christians are the only soldiers in the same army that fight against and kill their own. This is extremely appalling! Would you believe even the demons work together! They do not question the orders the devil gives them. How sad it is that the Body of Christ cannot work together! The demons probably laugh at us! The devil loves it when we disobey God and will not unify or be on one accord with each other. The demons even know that united we stand divided, we fall! Therefore, their job is to keep us divided, separated, and segregated! *Oh my God, help us!*

Let us bind together in unity and win the war of separation and segregation that our lives will give God glory!

Belt of Truth

So stand firm and hold your ground, HAVING TIGHTENED THE WIDE BAND OF TRUTH (personal integrity, moral courage) AROUND YOUR WAIST.

Truth defined is something that has actual existence, a fact.

You are of *your* father the devil, and it is your will to practice the desires [which are characteristic] of your father. He was a murderer from the

beginning and does not stand in the truth because there is no truth in him. When he lies, he
speaks what is natural to him, for he is a liar and
the father of lies *and* half-truths.

John 8:44 (AMP)

As we see, truth is the first piece of armor that was mention.
Lying is definitely a part of the BS. If we want to allow the BS,
the beastly spirit to prevail in our lives, then lie. Lying is one
of the worst things you can do. Proverbs 12:22 (AMP) puts it
like this: "Lying lips are extremely disgusting to the LORD, but
those who deal faithfully are His delight."

When we lie, the devil is getting the victory in our life.
He is the author of lying. He loves it when we tell lies. Lies
hurt. It is hard to find people that would just simply tell the
truth. What has happened to the truth? We see and hear lying
from the white house to the church house. Lies have caused
so many downfalls, divorces, murders, people locked up in a
prison that's innocent, employees have lost their jobs over a lie,
just to name a few things.

I know personally when I have lied, I felt horrible! It's one
of the worse feelings you can feel. The BS had taken me over! I
remember looking my mother right in her face and flat-footed
told a lie. Why? I asked myself that after I told the lie. I did
not hesitate to give a false answer. Was it worth it? *No!* Sometimes the lie is so small, like did you eat the last slice of cake or
did you leave the light on. Really, was it that serious that the
answer simply could have been, "Yes, I ate the cake?" A lie is a
lie, no matter how large or small it is. We do not think about it,
but what a small lie that results in a big consequence.

God looks at lying as repulsive! Lying is a sin, and sin reeks in God's nostrils. Lying must be horrible and revolting if the Bible says so. Psalm 101:7 (KJV): "He that worketh deceit shall not dwell within my house: he that telleth lies shall not tarry in my sight." *Wow*, that means a liar will not get a chance to stand before God in heaven because God already knows they are going to lie. Lying is just that horrific that it can cause eternal damnation!

Let us face it. We must have the Holy Spirit! What else will bring conviction to us when we are talking and fabricate a simple story.

Death and life are in the power of the tongue, and lying will certainly bring death.

Another situation happened. This time, I was lied to. I was working at an elementary school for about a month, and some of my co-workers knew that I once was a director and owned my own child care center.

First, let me preface this story by telling you that I was recovering from a catastrophic situation that caused great damage to my heart and my mind. I was in emotional recovery from an event that caused me to close my childcare center, which was a dream that had finally come true. You see, I always wanted to own a child care center since my youth. God opened the door for me to run and operate my childcare center for seven years. Within those seven years, I have seen the ups and downs of owning a business. But that year, things were beginning to look up. Increase in enrollment, I was working on receiving another star to be added to my star-rated center, we were serving six elementary schools, and I was busy! With the busyness of the business and being a wife, mother, and pastor's wife, and making sure that I did not put anything before God, my plate was full. I stayed before God on my knees, fasting and praying. I remember before I would go to work, I would drop my son off at school and head straight to the church to pray. Throughout the week, I would leave work and go to the church and get on the altar and pray. This was a special time for me because everything was shut out, and it was just me and God. There was no sound of busyness, it was just me and God. As time went on, I remember telling my office manager how tired I was. I was juggling so many balls. I was determined not to drop not one! I continued working.

In August 2016, I left work around 4:30 p.m. I continued my evening as usual. Little did I know that my life was getting ready to be changed forever! I heard the phone ring around midnight. When I answered, the man said, "This is Sergeant from the police department, I am trying to reach Evelyn Johnson." My heart began to race! He asked if I knew of a three-year-old child name *Xyz* that was enrolled at my center. I said yes. He then asked did I know where the child was because he never made it home. Immediately my husband got up because he could hear the officer on the speaker. I was shaking! My mouth was trembling so fast! I said, "Let me call the driver that was supposed to have dropped the child off at home." I called the driver, and she said, "I dropped him off at home," then when I said no, "You did not because I am on the phone with the police department and they are with the mother, and the mother said the child never made it home." She began to lie and said maybe he still at the center. I was on two phones, both on speaker, so the officer could hear what was being said. My mind was racing! I needed God like never before! My heart felt as if it was going to jump out of my chest! The child was not in the center, so the only other place would have been in the van!

Jesus, Help Me! Help!

My mind felt as if it was going to erupt because of the thought of the child in the van from 5 p.m to 1:00 a.m in ninety-degree heat in the hottest month of the year, the month of August, the outcome could not be a good one. In the meantime, my husband was getting dressed. He told me that he wanted to be the first responder to the center because if the child was in the van after eight hours in the hottest time of the day, he was probably dead. He told me he didn't want me to see that scene because, in most cases, the brain explodes from the heat. Faith stood up tall as a mountain inside my husband, and he made this statement, "I believe if the child is dead, I am going to pray and believe '*God to bring him back to life!*'"

After the initial shock, I came to myself! The Holy Spirit took over my mind! My mind was taken over with the Word of God from Jeremiah 32:27 (KJV) "Behold, I am the Lord, the God of all flesh: is there anything too hard for me?" I quote this verse all the time, and this time the Word talked to me! My demeanor changed. My faith told peace to take me over, and it did. My heart, mind, and soul were secure and assured in God.

I understand like never before why husbands and wives should be equally yoked and on one accord. I believed God too! Our faith gripped our total being and wrapped itself in an assurance that God is going to perform the supernatural and the child would live! I believe the Bible to be the infallible written Word of God! I believe God is the same yesterday, today, and forevermore! This day greater works had to be manifested!

My husband left before me. I remember as I was driving, all I could say was, "Jesus, Jesus, Jesus" over and over. I felt encased and coated with God's presence. It was like I was taken over by the Holy Spirit. There was no crying. The shaking was gone, and faith and trust drove me to my center.

When my husband got there, he said he went immediately to the seven-passenger van and opened the door on the right side and did not see the child. The child was not crying or screaming or anything, it was complete silence. My husband then went to the left side of the van and opened the door, and there the child was sitting in his car seat *alive! After eight hours of sitting in the van with no windows down, the child was alive!* He got the child out and asked him if he was okay, and the child said, "I am hungry"; other than that, the child being hungry, he had wet himself and had an understandable bowel movement.

The police met us at the center. They were mystified! They said they had never seen anything like this before! In most cases, after one or two hours, if a child is left in a vehicle in the heat, they would die. All glory goes to *God!* What a mighty indescribable God we serve!

When I arrived, I saw the child with my husband! I ran and picked him up and gave him a big hug full of love! I then went into the center to get him something to eat and drink. The employee met us there too. She was relieved that the child was alive as well. The officers asked me if I wanted to drive the child home, and I said yes. As I drove the child to his mother's house, I thanked my God all the way there! My soul was rejoicing in triumph victory that God had done it again! God had shown His magnificent power in the earth before all that was a witness!

When we arrived, the ambulance met us. The paramedics checked the child out and said he is fine! The paramedics said as they could tell there was nothing wrong with the child and that the mom needed to follow up with their doctor the next day and to make sure they give him lots of fluids. His mother was crying and telling me, "Thank you," and that she was sorry this had happened. I could not believe she was telling me she was sorry. I am the one that was extremely regretful that this event had happened.

After this traumatic event, I did not want the responsibility of another child's life on my hands. So, with much prayer, I submitted my letter to the childcare council stating that my center is closed indefinitely. I must admit that after I delivered the letter, I felt a weight lifted off me. It was like an elephant was sitting on me and got up! God knows what is best for us. Thank you, Lord.

As time went on, I ran into the child's mother in the store, and she said once again, "I am so sorry this happened to you" she kept apologizing to me, and I said, "No, I am the one that is sorry. Sorry was not enough words. I was sorry that my employee was neglectful and allowed this to happen." She said her son was fine and that they had followed up with his doctor, and they said he was fine also. I am so thankful for so many family and friends praying for us and checking on me during this harrowing time in my life. I will never forget one of my friends telling me, "God took the *heat* out of the *fire* for you!" When she said that, I envisioned throughout that day and night, the angels of the Lord surrounded the van with their feathers covering the van and the child from all hurt, harm, and danger.

The mother of this child was amazing throughout this whole situation. She did not press charges or try to sue me. She did not even press charges against the driver, our state automatically did that. The driver accepted full responsibility for all charges issued by the State Childcare Protective Services. My heart went out to my employee. I prayed for her because I know she did not mean to leave the child in the van. She had two small children of her own, so I know she must have felt grief-stricken. That was the last time I ever saw her.

At the next service at our church, my husband, pastor

Johnson encouraged the people to never stop praying because he believes because of the prayer life that I have and the love that I have for God and the faithful commitment, that God manifested His Word from James 5:16 (AMP) for me:

> The heartfelt *and* persistent prayer of a righteous man (believer) can accomplish much [when put into action and made effective by God—it is dynamic and can have tremendous power].

All the glory and praise go to our heavenly Father and our Lord and Savior Jesus Christ for what He has done!

Now back to the Belt of Truth school situation, as time went on, I only applied for part-time work because I knew I did not need to be overloaded in any area of my life until I recovered from that traumatic event. The weight of closing a business was enough all by itself. Believe me, when I tell you this, creditors do not care that a business closed for an unforeseen situation. All they want is their money. It was so much to deal with, but I know I was not alone God's power, mercy, and grace were with me. Thank you, Father, for never leaving me nor forsaking me.

Dear reader, now you know why I was in a tenuous and fragile state of mind. I just wanted to ease back into working with children without any demands. This is where the lie came in, one day state-licensed inspector came to conduct the annual inspection for the school. If you worked in any facility with children, the department of childcare regulations for your state could come and inspect your site without any notice. One of my co-workers, for no reason, went to our supervisor and told her that I called and reported the school to our state headquarters for childcare, and that was the reason why they were there to do an inspection. First of all, everybody knows that the inspector general for childcare licensing never lets anyone know when they are coming for an annual visit. My supervisor should have known that, but she was new at her job, and without hesitation, she believed the other worker because she had been working there longer than I had. When I was called into the office and questioned on this lying matter, my heart sunk. My face turned another color! I felt vandalized. It was as if my heart was burglarized from the truth. I was so hurt. I was more hurt than upset. It was a feeling that words cannot express! I could not understand for the life of me why she would lie on me. I did not know her. I had never seen her before in my life! What a way to start off a new job. All because of this lie, everyone was treating me differently. They were staring at me and whispering. If I came into the room, everyone immediately stopped talking. I know now she was operating in the BS. A lie is so damaging. Some people never recover from a lie.

The devil is a great deceiver! His goal is to make people think that there will be no consequences to lying.

The sad thing is the co-worker that lied felt no conviction. That is how the devil is; he has no conviction when he deceives us! He does not care about anyone! When he lies, he speaks what is natural to him, for he is a liar and the father of lies *and* half-truths! Remember, he hates us!

For the duration of my work time at the school, I did gain the trust of my supervisor and co-workers. The co-worker that lied continued to display depraved work ethics and ended up quitting. The saying is true a snake will always be a snake.

Therefore, we need the belt of truth on so when the BS spirit tries to stand up against the belt of truth, it will not win. It is like the belt-tightening up, causing us to think before answering; therefore, we will answer with the truth.

The outcome of a lie is never good when the truth is revealed.

> *But whatever [word] comes out of the mouth comes from the heart, and this is what defiles and dishonors the man.*

~ Die to Live... ~

Breastplate of Righteousness

And *having put on the breastplate of righteousness* (an upright heart).

Righteous defined as acting in accord with divine or moral law: free from guilt or sin.

The Bible says and having put on the breastplate of righteousness. That means it is up to us to do this. God is not going to put it on for you. He has given us the choice either to put it on or not. The breastplate of righteousness has been made available through Jesus Christ for anyone that believes in Him. Once the breastplate is put on, do not ever take it off.

The breastplate covers our torso, which is the area of the body that extends from the neck down to the pelvic area and does not include the arms. Isn't it interesting that the breastplate covers the heart? The heart is where our emotions, temperament the core of our feelings, live. The heart must be protected. Without the heart, there is no life physically, mentally, and spiritually.

He made Christ who knew no sin to [judicially] be sin on our behalf, so that in Him we would become the righteousness of God [that is, we would be made acceptable to Him and placed in a right relationship with Him by His gracious lovingkindness].

The breastplate of righteousness is the life that we are to live and the most important part of the armor. Jesus died for us to wear the breastplate of righteousness. What an indescribable price Jesus paid for us to live! Thank you, Jesus!

We cannot thank Jesus enough for becoming sin on our behalf. If Jesus had not died and risen with all power, there would be no righteousness, no *salvation*. With no righteousness or with no salvation, what would we need the rest of the armor for? When I think about all the things Jesus went through for me, my soul weeps with overwhelming love and thankfulness. My soul is saying, "Jesus, I don't want to hurt You again." I imagine in my mind that willfully sinning over and over is like stabbing and slapping Jesus in His face all over again! We are living in a time where holy and right living is grimace and frown upon. People say that's old fashion. They make jokes and make fun of people who are trying to live the way the Bible says. They say we do not have to live like that any longer. The sad thing is that some Christians think that way as well. This is a plot of the devil. Even in some churches, it is being taught that it's okay to sin. *Oh wow!* We all fall and sin, but it should not be a purposeful part of our life. The Bible is clear about holiness and righteousness, and never did it say that holiness was a denomination or organization, but it is a way of life for Christians, the saints of God.

Second Corinthians 5:21 (NIV) says: "God made him who had no sin to be sin for us, so that in him we might become the righteousness of God."

> For the grace of God has appeared that offers salvation to all people. It teaches us to say "No" to ungodliness and worldly passions, and to live self-controlled, upright and godly lives in this present age.

> Titus 2:11-12 (NIV)

God made Jesus, who had never sinned to be sin for us...what manner of love is this.

~ Die to Live...~

182

Ephesians 6:15 (EXB): "On your feet wear the Good News [Gospel] of peace to help you stand strong [for firm footing; *or* to be fully prepared]."

Ephesians 6:15 (AMP): "And having strapped on YOUR FEET THE GOSPEL OF PEACE IN PREPARATION [to face the enemy with firm-footed stability and the readiness produced by the good news]."

When I think of a strap or belt a band it is something that holds up a thing or secures it so it will not give way, become loose, or be lost.

If we do not strap, bind, and buckle ourselves down in the Word of God, the enemy could easily defeat us. The Word says to be firm footed and stable. If we are firm in our beliefs, nothing can shake us or cause us to change our minds. The amplified translation says, "We need to wear the Good News the gospel so we can stand strong and have firm footing and, most of all, be fully prepared." We always need to be ready to stand firm in the Word of God. Our minds need to be set and not willing to change from what the Word of God says.

Equip us, God! Train us, Father, in this war to walk the Word out in the name of Jesus!

One of the ways the devil defeats us is because we are not fully prepared in the Word of God.

The armor of God fits all together. The Word is our sword, our weapon, and if we do not know the Word or how to use our weapon, we are at a great disadvantage. That is like having a gun and do not know how to load it with bullets or how to pull the trigger! When the enemy comes, he got you! If we want to be ready when the enemy comes, then we must go to the spiritual gun range, which is the church, and learn how to shoot!

The Devil Is Analyzing Us

The devil studies us like a chess game. He watches and evaluates us. He has been on this earth since creation, so he knows how human beings behave and respond to certain situations. He watches and waits as he is constantly moving the prongs around on our chessboard of life. If we move too quickly without thinking, we make the wrong choice causing us to lose one of our pieces (peace, joy, faith, commitment, trust, right timing), this can go on and on. Your pieces are whatever in life we face.

~ Die to Live...~

Do Your Shoes Have Strings?

I noticed that none of the translations of Ephesians 6:15 (AMP) tells us to tie on our feet. It says, "And having strapped on YOUR FEET THE GOSPEL OF PEACE."

I believe it is because strings come to lose all the time. I see children and adults with their shoes untied, it is very noticeable. Well, it is also noticeable to others when we do not have our shoes strapped down being firm footed with the stability and the readiness produced by the good news. It is not good to be unprepared in any situation, especially in witnessing or teaching, preaching, etc., the Word of God.

Keep your shoes on and keep on walking and moving forward for God.

~ Die to Live...~

The Word Is Our Light

Psalm 119:105 (EXB): "Your Word is like a lamp for my feet and a light for my path [it shows how life should be lived]."

When we are in the dark and cannot see, it is our feet that bump into the object first. We cannot walk without our feet. When the lights are out, even in a familiar place, we still bump into things. We need light to see. We need the Word of God to see where to go, what to do, what to say even what to expect. Psalm 119:105 lets us know that we are on a path and the Word the lamp is to guide us, and we need the light to follow the path.

Jesus is the *light!* Jesus is our greatest example. He is the exemplary archetypal model of peace! Jesus's harmony of peace was even publicized on the cross as He committed Himself even to death.

When we have on the shoes of peace and walking and living like Jesus, we will be prepared and equipped to win the battles of life!

Illuminating of the Word brings Peace

Have you ever seen a spotlight? It is so bright that it illuminates what you are looking at. God's Word is so illuminating! It is so amazing when we need an answer from God, and He takes us to His Word and puts the spotlight right on the verse that we needed to answer the question or the situation that we are facing. The Word of God brings clarity and peace. God knew we would have battles in life, and we needed peace to win. It has been proven that the hothead, impetuous, impulsive person loses the fight. After all, they cannot reason levelheaded because they are not at peace within themselves.

Peace That Surpasses All Understanding

Peace is a sign and confirmation of assurance that we believe in God's Word.

We must keep our shoes of peace on because we never know what pathway in life will take us on.

I experienced Philippians 4:7 (EXB): "And God's peace, which is so great we cannot understand it [transcends/surpasses all comprehension], will keep [guard] your hearts and minds in Christ Jesus."

I never knew a peace like this before in my life! On November 27th, the day after my husband's birthday, death came to claim him. The Holy Spirit led my husband to have me anoint him with oil the week before the event took place. After I anointed him, he told me how he believed and wanted to please God, and if God did not touch and heal his body, this would be it for him on this earth. As we prayed together, the Holy Spirit filled the room. There was no doubt in my mind that God was not there with us. *Oh*, how I love praying. I know that might sound strange, but I really do. I love to dissolve, melt, and just liquefy in God's arms. I understand why the book of James tells us to pray fervently, earnestly, and with passion. I know it is not about a feeling, but I must admit I love the feeling the knowing that God's presence is in the room! There is a transformation that takes place in my mind, in my soul and spirit. I come out of prayer another way! I come out revived and refreshed with greater faith because the Holy Spirit bears witness to the Word and faith in God.

As we joined hands, our prayer request was incredibly detailed as we lifted his body, mind, and soul. He told me that the spirit of death had been following him around in the house. He said he would rebuke death, it would leave and then return again. My husband knew he was in a fight literally for his life.

He said he is not afraid of death. He understands that it is a vehicle that transports us to God, and Jesus has taken the sting out of death!

Before November 27th, about three weeks before, my husband came in the room and said, "I don't feel right. Get me a chair." I feel weird, and before he could finish what he was saying, he was out! His head had dropped. I called him, but I did not get a response. I told my son to get the anointing oil, and I anointed him and began to call on Jesus and prayed! He came back, but he could not speak! He had this glare in his eyes. It was like he was looking out into nothing. I kept calling on Jesus, and then I called my husband's name, believing that he would hear me! We yelled Jesus! Right then, I saw the power of God right before our eyes! He came back to himself and said he could hear us calling his name.

He told us later that it was like the cartoon show when you saw the spirit leave out of the roadrunner and someone pulled his legs back down into his body! He began to talk as nothing had happened. He felt very tired and weak. I stayed home from work the next day just to make sure he was okay.

As time went on and we continue our normal routine. My husband was supposed to schedule a doctor's follow-up appointment from the stroke he had earlier that year in July; that is another story. He kept putting it off because he was feeling better and Thanksgiving was approaching, and he said he did not want to spend the holiday in the hospital. This is where we catch up, we made it through Thanksgiving. I must say after the stoke and the last situation of him passing out, we look at holidays differently. To be honest, we look at every day differently! We do not know when we will take our last breath. We hear it all the time, "Cherish each day, make every minute count," but unfortunately, most of us do not until something tragic happens. You never know what you would do when the uncontrollable tragedies of life transpire. When the unforeseen horrific moment in life just takes you by surprise, what is in you will certainly come out.

Now, back to Tuesday, November 27th, the day after his birthday at 6:25 a.m., my son and I were getting ready for the day. I was in the bathroom when I heard my husband coming up the stairs. What got my attention was he was breathing so hard and loud panting that it made me come out of the bathroom to ask, "Are you okay?" He had gone downstairs to warm up something to eat even though he was asked not to go downstairs without one of us with him. As soon as he made it to the top, he took one step and fell out! I began calling his name! No response! I told my son to call 911! In the meantime, I rolled him over, still calling his name, no response! I called my Godmother, who is a prayer warrior, to pray as I had her on speakerphone. My husband came back! I told him not to move and that the ambulance was on the way! My husband is a private man and comes from old-school teaching. His mother told him never to leave the house without good clean underwear on because you never know if you might have to go to the hospital. My husband said he was wearing his sleeping bleached-out underwear, and he was not going to the hospital with them on. He was so concerned about having on good clean underwear he said, "Son, go get me some good underwear." I was outdone! Here he is can hardly breathe worrying about underwear! I said, "Son, don't worry about that!" He said, "Son, do what I said to do!" Needless to say, my son went and got him some good underwear. We were able to switch them, but as soon as we were finished, he was out again. No response! I brought this up for parents to know what you teach your children they will remember.

The paramedics were at the house; it took about six minutes for them to get there! It was about six of them that came in, and they began asking me questions. I told them he had a stroke in July and back surgery prior. They wanted to know if he was taken pain pills. I said, "Yes," assessing the situation they thought maybe it could have been an overdose from the pain pills. My husband came back to himself, and they were able to ask him more questions as he was talking, and he passed out again! I asked the paramedics if he was alive, and they said yes. They took him out of the house with just his underclothes and a blanket. It was about twenty degrees outside.

All during this time, I had such peace as we continued to pray and finished getting dressed to meet them at the hospital. I called my mom and told her what was going on and to pray. I sent out a group text to my church prayer group. These prayer warriors have been praying every Wednesday for our pastor faithfully for over fifteen years. A group text was sent out throughout the USA to family and friends to pray. We are so thankful that we are surrounded by prayer warriors.

We made it to the hospital about thirty minutes later. He was in the emergency room being seen by doctors. One of the Elders from the church came in and prayed for the pastor, which to this day, he does not remember him coming to see him.

After hours of being there, my son and I were able to leave to go and get something to drink. Since it was Tuesday, this was perfect timing for me to join the conference prayer line with my mother and the prayer warriors at my home church in Florida. God's timing is amazing! As I looked out the window, I saw gentle soft snow falling to the ground as my heartbeat was the same. Soft quiet beats of faith in God calmed my soul. I joined in on the call, the warriors were already praying for my husband. I normally pray as well, but this time I was on the receiving end. After the prayer, they asked how he was doing. I told them I was still waiting to hear from the doctor on what the diagnose would be. They begin to rejoice and thank God because he was still alive!

Visitation from God

In the ambulance from the ride from our house to the hospital, my husband had a visitation from God. He said it was dark, dark black. A blackness that he has never seen, but he said it was not scary darkness. It was a quietness, a peace he had never felt or experienced. He asked God, "Is this it? Am I dead?" He then said, "Evelyn, I love you; Son, I love you." He said nothing on this earth mattered anymore. Everything was wiped away. No worries or thoughts came to his mind of his family, the church, bills, etc., nothing in the natural crossed his mind, right then he released himself, gave up, he surrendered. As soon as he surrendered, he heard the paramedics say, "We got him back! He is breathing!" Then he said, "I can't breathe! I can't breathe!" When he woke up, he was in the emergency room.

I can see in the spiritual realm that when my husband gave up and surrendered, that is when God stepped in and rescued, saved him. When we surrender to God, He will step in and help us as well.

On the third day in the hospital, my husband had another visitation from God. He said God showed him things and told him things. He told God, "I don't want to go back the same. If I go back, use me for greater signs and wonders." He told God he wanted to lead souls to Christ in great numbers and that he no longer wanted to be the same man, the same father, the same preacher, or pastor. God showed him things in the future. His experience, he said, assured him that God is real and death is real. He said that he wanted to tell everyone he encounters that when death comes, there is nothing you can do but surrender.

It Takes Faith to Wait

The wait was long in the emergency room area. We waited from 6:30 am until 2 p.m. to get a room. The reason being is because they said they could not figure out what was wrong with him. The doctors said they tested him for heart attack, stroke, etc., and just could not pinpoint the problem. I remember walking past the nurse's station, and one of the nurses asked me, "How is the mystery man?" and I said, "Mystery man, what do you mean?" She said, "The doctors tested him for everything they could think of, and they concluded that he is a mystery to them," but the main doctor said, "I am not going to give up until I figure this out." Right here, I see this as the favor of God watching out for him. Thank you, Jesus!

All during this time, I was calm. I did not have any anxiety at all. I knew the Holy Spirit was at work. Sometimes when I am going through a hard time or waiting on a result, my stomach is in knots. I feel extremely nervous, but not this time. I patiently waited with a knowing that God was in control. Finally, the doctor came in and said, "I had to do just one more test. I wanted to x-ray his lungs." After X-raying his lungs, he diagnosed him with bilateral pulmonary embolism, PE, in each lung. This was the cause of him passing out! He was not getting enough air to his lungs!

As believers, we can see God's hand in everything. How he got the PE was from a blood clot stemming from the stroke he had. The clot started in his leg and traveled up to his lungs. During the recovery from the stroke, the doctors had put him on blood thinners. This is where I see God working things out for his good, if he had not had the blood thinners, the clots could have moved quicker from his leg to the lungs and killed him.

We experienced this firsthand.

> And we know [with great confidence] that God
> [who is deeply concerned about us] causes all

things to work together [as a plan] for good for those who love God, to those who are called according to His plan *and* purpose.

Romans 8:28 (AMP)

If my husband had waited to go downstairs once we had left the house and passed out without anyone being there, he would have died! The stroke that he had, the doctor said, "If it could be said a "good place" to have a stroke, he had it in the best spot." We are so thankful for God's grace and mercy! Truly all things work together for our good!

~ Die to Live... ~

Shield of Faith –

See Chapter "The Combative Beast Against Faith" for more on faith.

Ephesians 6:16 (AMP) says: "Above all, lift up the [protective] shield of faith with which you can extinguish all the flaming arrows of the evil *one*."

"*Faith* is the *invisible shield* that *fights a*ll the things *visible* and *non-visible*" (Pastor Johnson).

We need every piece of the armor of God, we especially need the shield of faith. We are in a daily fight, and for us to keep our minds, our prayer request, our trust, the Word consistency in our heart, we need the shield of faith to protect the fiery darts of the devil. Why do you think the Word tells us above all to lift the shield of faith? Above everything else, *believe*! Faith is belief and total trust in God. Faith is so powerful that the devil does not want us to believe God because he knows God can do anything. Faith is a powerful weapon.

Faith works! If faith did not work, why would the devil and the BS our flesh fight so hard against it? My pastor once said, "Faith is the glue that holds everything together, and if you do not have faith, who are you praying to?" How true this statement is. Think about this; how can we say we believe in God and then do not believe in the things we are asking for? Faith is faith for everything. Faith is the only thing that will hold our prayer request together until it comes to pass.

Faith is so *powerful* that the devil arms himself not with a regular dart but with fiery darts! Darts that are flaming red hot, burning, blazing, scorching, and on fire trying to make sure he *put out our faith*! Remember, he knows God, and he is trying everything in his power to keep us from believing and trusting in the all-powerful, all-knowing God and His Word. Faith Works!

And also [in addition to all this; or in all circumstances] use the shield of faith with which you can stop [extinguish] all the burning arrows [fiery darts] of the Evil One (EXB).

Keep Your Shield up

One way the devil gets us is that we take our faith shield down. Faith is now, at that very moment, currently. How long is yours now? We must believe until something happens. We cannot stop believing in the middle of the prayer request, which is considered to be doubting. Too many times, we start off believing while we are in church or with someone that is praying for us, our faith is strong, but what happens when we do not get our desired result right then? We sometimes doubt, or we say, "God must not have wanted me to have that or get that, or maybe it was not God will." We make up all kinds of excuses to assist doubt when we do not get what we want and when we want it.

Now Faith Is Faith until Your Now Happens

It is time to have *faith beyond the here and now! Keep believing! No matter what, believe!*

Faith is in the right now, not later or in the maybe it is at that very moment, second. When faith encounters Jesus, there will be an immediate result. The manifestation may not be revealed every time in the same manner, but know the connection was made, and the outcome will be revealed. Believe!

Do not let anything or anyone take your faith away because doubt cancels faith right out! Friends let us be armed and dangerous with our faith.

When the devil shoots his fiery darts, hold up your shield that reads "I believe!" You are more than a conquer!

~ Die to Live...~

Sword Word of the Spirit

"And the sword of the Spirit, which is the Word of God." (Ephesians 6:16)

The Word of God

There is no way we are going to win the fight of our life without the Word of God, which is our sword. God has equipped us with the most powerful weapon on this earth. The Word.

Jesus Is the Word Our Sword

In the beginning [before all time] was the Word (Christ), and the Word was with God, and the Word was God Himself. He was [continually existing] in the beginning [co-eternally] with God.

John 1:1-2 (AMP)

Before anything was Christ Jesus, the Word was. And if Jesus is our Sword, how can we lose a battle or a war? Jesus said,

I told you these things so that you can have peace in me. In this world, you will have trouble [persecution; suffering], but be brave [take courage/heart]! I have defeated [victory over; conquered; overcome] the world.

John 16:33 (EXB)

Jesus has defeated everything in this world! If we believe Jesus is the Word then we should read it, live it, and then "do Jesus!" James 1:22 (EXB): "Do what God's teaching says; when you only listen and do nothing, you are fooling yourselves [Be doers of the word, and not only hearers, deceiving yourselves."

I pose a question of how can we say we love Jesus and do not love the Word? *Hmmm*…something to think about.

The Word is extremely powerful and valuable that Matthew 24:35 (KJV) says: "Heaven and earth shall pass away, but my words shall not pass away." How can the Word pass away if the Word is Jesus? Readers, we can rest assured that the Word is true, the Word is Jesus the Word is:

> For the word of God is living and active *and* full of power [making it operative, energizing, and effective]. It is sharper than any two-edged sword, penetrating as far as the division of the soul and spirit [the completeness of a person], and of both joints and marrow [the deepest parts of our nature], exposing *and* judging the very thoughts and intentions of the heart.

> Hebrews 4:12 (AMP):

The fight for our soul is the most important fight we will ever fight on this earth. In war, there will be death. We need a weapon that will kill. The sharp Word will kill our flesh, our will, and our way. The Word will cut down, chop in half, destroy the BS and anything the enemy the devil comes after us with. The tempter who is the devil tried to tempt Jesus in the wilderness and Jesus the Word himself used the powerful Word on the devil But Jesus replied, "It is written *and* forever remains written, 'MAN SHALL NOT LIVE BY BREAD ALONE, BUT BY EVERY WORD THAT COMES OUT OF THE MOUTH OF GOD'" (Matthew 4:4, AMP).

> All Scripture is God-breathed [given by divine inspiration] and is profitable for instruction, for conviction [of sin], for correction [of error

and restoration to obedience], for training in righteousness [learning to live in conformity to God's will, both publicly and privately—behaving honorably with personal integrity and moral courage]; so that the man of God may be complete *and* proficient, outfitted *and* thoroughly equipped for every good work.

2 Timothy 3:16-17 (AMP)

The Word is an armament, a weapon. If we use the Word, we will be victorious in every area of our lives. The Word gives us hope, the Word gives us answers to every situation or problem we will ever face. The Word is our weapon to show us how to combat and beat the BS, the beastly spirit, our flesh that fights against God.

The Mighty Powerful Word gives us the following:

Instruction—(instruct)—to give the knowledge to *teach, train.* The Word teaches and trains us how to be like Jesus. How to live a sanctified set apart life pleasing to God.

But the Helper (Comforter, Advocate, Intercessor—Counselor, Strengthener, Standby), the Holy Spirit, whom the Father will send in My name [in My place, to represent Me and act on My behalf], He will teach you all things. And He will help you remember everything that I have told you.

John 14:26 (AMP)

Conviction—(convict)—to find or prove to be guilty. The Word will inform us and convict us when we sin and show us what is offensive to God.

> But I tell you the truth, it is to your advantage that I go away; for if I do not go away, the Helper (Comforter, Advocate, Intercessor—Counselor, Strengthener, Standby) will not come to you; but if I go, I will send Him (the Holy Spirit) to you [to be in close fellowship with you]. And He, when He comes, will **convict** the world about [the guilt of] sin [and the need for a Savior], and about righteousness, and about judgment: about sin [and the true nature of it], because they do not believe in Me [and My message]; about righteousness [personal integrity and godly character], because I am going to My Father and you will no longer see Me; about judgment [the certainty of it], because the ruler of this world (Satan) has been judged *and* condemned.

> John 16:7-11 (AMP)

Correction—(correct)—to make or set right: *amend* to put right. The Word will correct us when we are wrong. We need correction. How would we know if we are wrong if there is no correction? Job 5:17 (EXB): "The one whom God corrects [reproves] is happy [blessed], so do not hate being corrected by [reject/despise the instruction of] the Almighty."

Conformity to God's Will—(conform) to be obedient or compliant. For our sword, the Word, to be effective in our lives, we must do the will of God. We must submit to God's will and His way. We can be assured that God's will is always the best for us in every area of our lives. Matthew 6:10 (EXB): "May your kingdom come and what you want [Your will] be done, here on earth as it is in heaven." The flesh wants to fight against the will of God but does not give in to your flesh. If we want to please God and live in victory, comply with God's will.

Equipping—(equip) to make ready: *prepare* to make ready beforehand for some purpose, use, or activity. The Word will equip and prepare us for life's journey that we will make it to our destination, which is heaven.

> "But be on guard, so that your hearts are not weighed down *and* depressed with the giddiness of debauchery and the nausea of self-indulgence and the worldly worries of life, and then that day [when the Messiah returns] will not come on you suddenly like a trap; for it will come upon all those who live on the face of all the earth. But keep alert at all times [be attentive and ready], praying that you may have the strength *and* ability [to be found worthy and] to escape all these things that are going to take place, and to stand in the presence of the Son of Man [at His coming]."

Luke 21:34-36 (AMP)

Training— (train)— to teach to make fit, qualified, or proficient, to form by instruction, discipline, or drill.

God gave us the Word, so we will make it back to Him. God's Word will make us fit for the kingdom of God and qualify and make us proficient in the earth. Second Timothy 3:17 (AMP) says: "So that the man of God may be complete *and* proficient, outfitted *and* thoroughly equipped for every good work."

Psalm 144:1(EXB): "Praise [Blessed be] the LORD, my Rock, who trains me [my hands] for war, who trains me [my fingers] for battle."

Dear reader, God loves us so much that He has given us everything we need through Jesus Christ the Word of God. Hold on to the sword, the Word that cannot be defeated!

Hallelujah! Thank you, Lord, for training us in life's war to win!

~ Die to Live...~

Be Consistent or the Beast Will Win

As we come closer to the end of this book, the bottom line of the summation is that we must die to live. The flesh, the will of the flesh, the sinful nature of who we are must be terminated. A victorious life is guaranteed to us if we live and perform the Will of God and stay consistent in our faith and trust in Him.

"Consistent: showing steady conformity to character, profession, belief, or custom a *consistent* patriot." (Merriam Webster)

Being consistent, stable, and obedient is hard for a lot of people. I do not know if it is because we get bored or cannot stay focus, but I do know it is a struggle. Just think how far along we would be if we were consistent and committed to the betterment of ourselves in the natural, even more so in the spiritual. Our prayer life, reading and studying, meditating, and our walk with God would be enhanced like never before. The definition of consistent is showing steady conformity to character, belief. If we stay consistent, firmly fixed, and immoveable in our submission to embrace the character of Christ Jesus and our belief and faith in God, we will defeat our flesh the BS.

Consistent in being Faithful

Faithful—adhering firmly and devotedly, as to a per-

son, cause, or idea; loyal. Responsible; conscientious—
(noun) one who is faithful: a loyal follower or member.
Synonyms: constant, dedicated, devoted, steadfast, true,
loyal (Dictionary.com).

Antonyms: disloyal, faithless, false, fickle, inconstant, per-
fidious, recreant, traitorous, treacherous, unfaithful, untrue.

Faithful implies unwavering adherence to a person or thing
or to the oath or promise by which a tie was contracted.

"*Loyal* implies a firm resistance to any temptation to desert
or betray" (Merriam Webster).

In the kingdom of God, we use the word faithful. Faithfulness is up at the top of the list with God. We must stay
faithful, true, and dedicated to our confession of faith in
Jesus. When we accepted Jesus as our Lord and Savior, we
should not allow our flesh to make us disloyal and unfaithful
no matter what we are suffering or going through. God rewards faithfulness. Revelation 2:10[b] (EXB): "But be faithful,
even if you have to die, and I will give you the crown [[c]a wreath
worn to indicate high status or as a reward] of life."

We want our faithfulness to be relentless. Our devotion
and loyalty to God and His Word must be persistent. This
scripture is telling us that no matter what we must stay faithful
even if it cost your life. Being faithful is so essential to God
that the faithful Christian will receive a reward, a wreath to be
worn indicating high status of faithfulness to God. How marvelous is that! Everyone in heaven will know you were faithful
on earth. Being faithful matters to God, and it should matter
to us, let us stay steadfast and loyal to being faithful so we will
not desert or betray God in our commitment to Him.

Be Consistent in Our Walk

But I say, walk *habitually* in the [Holy] Spirit [seek Him and be responsive to His guidance], and then you will certainly not carry out the desire of the sinful nature [which responds impulsively without regard for God and His precepts]. For the sinful nature has its desire which is opposed to the Spirit, and the [desire of the] Spirit opposes the sinful nature; for these [two, the sinful nature and the Spirit] are in direct opposition to each other [continually in conflict], so that you [as believers] do not [always] do whatever [good things] you want to do.

Galatians 5:16-17 (AMP)

So I tell you: Live [Walk] by following [guided by; in the power of; by] the Spirit. Then you will not do what your sinful self [sinful nature; flesh] wants [desires; craves]. Our sinful self [sinful nature; flesh] wants [desires] what is against the Spirit, and the Spirit wants [desires] what is against our sinful self [sinful nature; flesh]. [For] The two are against [opposed to; *or* hostile toward] each other, so you cannot do just what you please [want].

Galatians 5:16-17 (EXB)

In these verses, we are getting knowledge of how to spiritually die. The word habitually stands out. We know that habit is the root word of habitual. We have so many habits, things that we do routinely every single day. If we get in the habit to walk or live consistently in the Holy Spirit that is pursued after Him and be receptive and alert to His direction, leadership, and control, then we will cancel out the craving of our flesh, our sinful nature. The sinful nature is evil, bad, wicked, and corrupt! We have seen and experienced the outcome of carrying out the desires of the flesh, and it's not good. If only we would have just listened to the Holy Spirit tugging at our hearts and mind, we would not be in some of the situations that we are in now or have experienced. Why didn't we just adhere? Why didn't we just follow or obey the Holy Spirit? We said, "Something told me to do this or that," and after we make the wrong decision, we then say, "That something was the Holy Spirit." Let us yield and accept the leading of the Holy Spirit, so we can always receive the best results.

The Beast is the Sinful Nature

Those who live following their sinful selves [sinful nature; flesh] think only about [have their minds set on; *or* have their outlook shaped by] things that their sinful selves [sinful nature; flesh] want.

Romans 8:5 (EXB)

Think about this: if the wages of sin is death, and if we think, act, do, make decisions from our sinful flesh, could it be that we are bringing death to whatever we are doing? If something is dead, how can it bring forth life? How can a dead body bring another dead body back to life? We need the Holy Spirit to live in us to be made alive.

But those who live following the Spirit are thinking about [have their minds set on; *or* have their outlook shaped by] the things the Spirit wants them to do [of the Spirit]. If people's thinking is controlled by [*or* outlook/mind is set on] the sinful self [sinful nature; flesh], there is [the result is] death. But if their thinking is controlled by [*or* outlook/mind is set on] the Spirit, there is [the result is] life and peace. **7** When people's thinking is controlled by [*or* outlook/mind is set on] the sinful self [sinful nature; flesh], they are against [hostile to] God, because they refuse to obey [submit to] God's law and really are not even able to obey [submit to] God's law. Those people who are ruled by [*or* under the control of; in] their sinful selves [their sinful nature; the flesh] cannot please God. But you are not ruled by [controlled by; *or* in] your sinful selves [your sinful nature; the flesh], but by [*or* in] the Spirit, if that Spirit of God really lives in you. But the person who does not have the Spirit of Christ does not belong to Christ. Your body will always be [is] dead because of sin. But if Christ is in you, then the Spirit gives you [is] life, because Christ made you right with God [of righteousness]. God raised Jesus from the dead, and if God's Spirit is living in you, the One who raised Christ from the dead will also give life to your mortal bodies that die, through his Spirit who lives in you. So, my brothers and sisters, we must not be ruled by [are not obligated to] our sinful selves [our sinful nature; the flesh] or live the way our sinful selves want [according to the sinful nature/flesh]. **13** [For] If you use your lives to do the wrong things your sinful selves want [live according to the flesh], you will die spiritually [die]. But if you use the Spirit's help to [by the Spirit] stop doing the wrong things you do with [put to death the deeds of] your body, you will have true life [live].

Romans 8:5-13 (EXB)

When our flesh is dead. The beastly spirit, our flesh cannot bring forth any life, as stated earlier. For us not to be controlled and ruled by our beastly spirit, we must have and use the Holy Spirit to help us deny sin. Just like alcohol, cocaine, heroin, etc., open the door for demonic attacks, the Holy Spirit is the door opener for us to God and the things of God. The Holy Spirit is the prescription we want to have! We want to be addicted to You, God, in Jesus's name.

~ Die to Live…~

The Combative Beast
Against Faith

Faith brings life to words…

Our flesh battles with faith because we want to see in order to believe.

"The apostles said to the Lord, 'Increase our faith [our ability to confidently trust in God and in His power]'" (Luke 17:5, AMP).

Merriam dictionary defines *faith* as belief and trust in and loyalty to God, firm belief in something for which there is no proof, complete trust, something that is believed especially with strong conviction.

> Now faith is the assurance (title deed, confirmation) of things hoped for (divinely guaranteed), and the evidence of things not seen [the conviction of their reality—faith comprehends as fact what cannot be experienced by the physical senses].

> Hebrews 11:1 (AMP)

The title of Hebrews eleventh chapter is "The Triumphs of Faith."

How appropriate and most fitting this title is for this chapter. Faith trumps everything! Faith triumphs over doubt, fear, sickness, disease, lack, whatever exists or can exist faith will give us victory in every situation in life.

This is the most crucial fight and struggles we will have in life; the fight against ourselves, our mind the flesh to believe and trust God without a doubt.

> But without faith, it is impossible to [walk with God and] please Him, for whoever comes [near] to God must [necessarily] believe that God exists and that He rewards those who [earnestly and diligently] seek Him.

Hebrews 11:6 (AMP)

The devil will fight us to the end for us not to believe in God and not to believe in Jesus and the Word. He knows that doubt will cancel everything out. Hebrews tells us that without faith, it is *not* possible and ridiculous for us to think that we can please God. We must have unblemished and flawless faith and belief in God. There cannot be a spec of doubt in our faith. God has assured us in The Word of His great power and that He can do anything but fail.

When we doubt, we completely cancel out what we are believing God for, it does not matter how long we might have been praying, asking for whatever it is doubt will put a stop to the response. I believe it insults God when we doubt Him. What we are saying is that we do not believe that God is all-powerful and that He can do whatever it is that we are praying for. Second Corinthians 5:7 (KJV) says: "For we walk by faith, not by sight." If we can just get to the point that we believe God without seeing it first, then we have won the faith battle.

"Jesus said to him, 'Because you have seen Me, do you now believe? Blessed [happy, spiritually secure, and favored by God] are they who did not see [Me] and yet believed [in Me]'" (John 20:29, AMP).

No Matter What Keep Believing

One of the most encouraging faith stories in the Bible for me is the woman with the issue of blood:

> A woman [in the crowd] had [suffered from] a hemorrhage for twelve years, and had endured much [suffering] at the hands of many physicians. She had spent all that she had and was not helped at all, but instead had become worse. She had heard [reports] about Jesus, and she came up behind Him in the crowd and touched His outer robe. For she thought, "If I just touch His clothing, I will get well." Immediately her flow of blood was dried up; and she felt in her body [and knew without any doubt] that she was healed of her suffering.
>
> Mark 5:25-29 (AMP)

Immediately Jesus, recognizing in Himself that power had gone out from Him, turned around in the crowd and asked, "Who touched My clothes?" His disciples said to Him, "You see the crowd pressing in around You [from all sides], and You ask, 'Who touched Me?'" He kept looking around to see the woman who had done it. And the woman, though she was afraid and trembling, aware of what had happened to her, came and fell down before Him and told Him the whole truth. Then He said to her, "Daughter, your faith [your personal trust and confidence in Me] has restored you to health; go in peace and be [permanently] healed from your suffering."

Have you ever been in a situation where you tried everything, and things just got worse? This is what happened to the woman with the issue of blood. First, she had to acknowledged that she needed help beyond what man could do because she had tried everything. She needed a miracle.

Do you need a miracle today?

Here we see where faith goes beyond what you know. The woman did not know Jesus. She was not one of Jesus's followers, she had only heard about Him and believed! Faith comes by hearing and hearing the Word, and who is the Word? Jesus is the Word.

> In the beginning [before all-time] was the Word (Christ), and the Word was with God, and the Word was God Himself.
>
> And the Word (Christ) became flesh, and lived among us; and we [actually] saw His glory, glory as belongs to the [One and] only begotten *Son* of the Father, [the Son who is truly unique, the only One of His kind, who is] full of grace and truth (absolutely free of deception).
>
> John 1:1,14 (AMP)

This woman was desperate! So desperate that she did not care who was around her, who was looking at her, how she looked or smelled, she knew she needed Jesus. We, too, must press our way through doubt and fear and just believe! She pressed, and faith touched Jesus! Look what the Word said, "Immediately her flow of blood was dried up, and she felt in her body [and knew without any doubt] that she was healed of her suffering!"

Faith is instant! She *knew*! She *believed*! Without *any doubt*! She was *healed*!

Faith is in the right now, not later or in the maybe it is at that very moment, second. When faith encounters Jesus, there will be an immediate result. The manifestation may not be revealed every time in the same manner, but know the connection was made, and the outcome will be revealed. Believe.

What is so amazing about faith there is no limit or time frame that you must be in to use it. This is a good place to thank God for giving everyone faith. Everyone has it rather they use it or not, it is there. Faith is so powerful! When the woman touched Jesus, He said to her, "Daughter, your faith [your personal trust and confidence in Me] has restored you to health; go in peace and be [permanently] healed from your suffering." Her faith, her personal trust, and her confidence in Jesus healed her. A lot of times, we want other people to pray for us when we are in need or in a crisis, but faith is personal trust. Just like we must work out our own soul salvation, we have to have our own individual faith. There is nothing wrong with having others join in with us in faith, but for faith connection to work, that individual must have faith also. The Word tells us in Matthew 9:29 (AMP), "Then He touched their eyes, saying, 'According to your faith [your trust and confidence in My power and My ability to heal] it will be done to you.'"

According to your faith…

We must believe bottom line. Because of faith, this woman

was healed permanently, for good. Because of faith, we, too, can be healed and our prayers answered. Thank you, Jesus.

Another example of great faith is the centurion. He had so much faith in Jesus that he knew that if Jesus just spoke the Word his servant would be healed. Jesus was amazed at that type of faith! Let us also amaze God with our faith.

> As Jesus went into Capernaum, a centurion came up to Him, begging Him [for help], and saying, "Lord, my servant is lying at home paralyzed, with intense *and* terrible, tormenting pain." Jesus said to him, "I will come and heal him." But the centurion replied to Him, "Lord, I am not worthy to have You come under my roof, but only say the word, and my servant will be healed. For I also am a man subject to authority [of a higher rank], with soldiers subject to me; and I say to one, 'Go!' and he goes, and to another, 'Come!' and he comes, and to my slave, 'Do this!' and he does it." When Jesus heard this, He was amazed and said to those who were following Him, "I tell you truthfully, I have not found such great faith [as this] with anyone in Israel.

> Matthew 8:5-10 (AMP)

The BS, beastly spirit will fight against the unseen. Our flesh wants to be in control and wants to see before believing. I think about the saying, "I am from Missouri, the show me state." We want to see first, but that is not faith. This combative beast just will not give up. The beast of the flesh is very argumentative with the Holy Spirit. The Holy Spirit will bear witness of the Word of God, and the BS will argue with it. We do not see it as arguing, but the meaning of arguing is to give evidence. The Holy Spirit gives us evidence in the Word, and yet we doubt God.

Romans 10:17 (ESV) says: "So faith comes from hearing, and hearing through the word of Christ." When doubt and uncertainty overwhelm our minds, we need to read the Word. What are you listening to? Who has your ear? I do not know about you, but it seems like if doubt is knocking on the door of my mind, it's because I am listening to someone or something that is not lining up with the Word of God. Sometimes people do not mean any harm, but they give you their opinions and their advice, and it changes what you were believing depending on who is talking to you. If it is someone you value their words, then it will have a bigger effect on your mind because you respect them and let us not forget that words have power.

This is dangerous because the Bible says: "Not at all! Let God be true, and every human being a liar. As it is written: 'So that you may be proved right when you speak and prevail when you judge'" (Romans 3:4, NIV)

I know people that will believe what someone has told them over what the Word of God says. Once again, this is extremely dangerous because they are putting that person above God. We must fight for our faith even if it is against ourselves. Do not let the BS win!

No Matter What, Keep Believing!

No matter what you are facing, no matter what the need might be, please know that God is able to do your *it*, whatever the *it* is; *God* is *greater*!

Faith scriptures to hide in your heart:

Luke 1:37 (ESV): "For nothing will be impossible with God.

Mark 9:23 (ESV): "And Jesus said to him, 'If you can'! All things are possible for one who believes."

John 14:14 (KJV): "If ye shall ask any thing in my name, I will do it."

~ Die to Live... ~

The Powerful Weapon of Prayer

First Thessalonians 5:17 (NLT) "Never stop praying."

We have a powerful weapon that has no limits to it, this weapon was paid in full on Calvary by our Savior Jesus Christ. It is given to everyone that accepts Jesus as Savior. This weapon called prayer gives us unlimited access to our Father, God. We get to choose which prayer weapon we want to have, you can choose a BB gun, shotgun, raffle, nine mm, or a four hundred sixty-magnum prayer weapon! Our weapon is determined on our prayer life. If we give God a little time in prayer, we are armed with a BB gun. If we pray without ceasing, we are loaded with a four hundred sixty magnum! We need prayer in our lives for the BS, the beast to die and stay dead. We must stay in continued prayer. There is so much to prayer. Not only do we get to talk to God, causing us to gain a closer relationship, but we get information, insight, revelation, wisdom, direction, answers to questions, etc., we also get peace, mental therapy, soundness of thought, joy, and the list goes on. I do not know what I would do without prayer. Prayer is one of my getaways from the stresses in life. Prayer is more potent than we will ever realize. I understand more and more why we must pray without ceasing. We must pray regardless of what is going on in our lives, regardless of how we feel, we must pray no matter what because of the warfare, the fight that we face continuously, throughout the day. The flesh nor the devil ever takes a break! This is just one reason why we must pray and be filled and led by the Holy Spirit. We must stay connected to the Holy Spirit no matter what. We need the power of God; we need to know what God's Will is on a day-to-day basis. We get that power through the Holy Spirit.

Prayer is our *powerful weapon*!

> Therefore, confess your sins to one another [your false steps, your offenses], and pray for one another, that you may be healed and restored. The heartfelt *and* persistent prayer of a righteous man (believer) can accomplish much [when put into action and made effective by God—it is dynamic and can have tremendous power].

> James 5:16 (AMP)

When we are ardent, sincere, and persistent, relentless, and consistent in prayer, the scripture says that a righteous person that is a believer in Jesus their prayer will accomplish much because it is made effective and successful by God. I want my prayer to have great power! I want to live a life pleasing to God so that when I pray, mountains move! Sickness is eradicated! Souls are saved and set free from whatever is binding them! I want to be able to pray when my flesh is out of control and tell it to cease, and it does!

Have you ever wondered why we are greatly fought against when it comes to prayer? Have you ever wondered why the prayer groups are the smallest in every church regardless of the size of the church? The question could be asked why something so small as just saying words would be so hard? There must be something about death and life in the power of our tongues (Proverbs 18:21).

Prayer is our secret weapon, and the devil knows this, and he will try to do whatever is necessary to keep us from praying. He knows prayer attached with faith and the Word of God is dynamic power! Stay powerful and pray!

We talk all day long! Some people even talk in their sleep. We can find almost anything to talk about, I even know people that if it is quiet for a minute, they will make up something to talk about because they just got to talk, *lol*! But when it is time to talk to God the mouth, the vocal cords shut down. We should know the devil is at work! It is God's will that we pray and talk to Him. The closer we get to God, the closer God will get to us.

This is something else to think about you can find people in church singing in the choir, ushering, teaching all types of classes, doing whatever it takes to be on the praise and worship team, volunteer to be on committees, nursery workers, drivers, parking attendants, kitchen ministry, whatever ministry is in the church you will find people on it, but when the call is made for prayer the sign-up list is empty or few names, the pews are empty, etc. all because of war! The war is between the flesh, the BS, the beast fighting against the Holy Spirit! It isn't that people don't know that they need to pray, they do, but the fight is so great with the BS the beastly spirit that they give in to the BS, no matter how many messages pastors preach, no matter how many books they might read and most importantly the Word of God tells us to but they still won't give over to prayer. This baffles me because God is wanting to have a closer relationship with His children, and they stay far away.

There must be something to this orison call prayer...

Could it be because of the great power and results that come from prayer? Could it be because we get to hear from God, and He hears us?

The devil does not want us to be powerful, knowledgeable, and in constant fellowship with God, so he does whatever it takes to keep us from praying! If you think about it what is so hard about simply talking to God? The devil put thoughts in people's minds that you have to pray grand prayers or be skillful in your prayer. I have never read in the Bible that we have to be skillful when praying or that we must dot every "i" and cross every "t." I have read in Jeremiah 29:12-13 (AMP) saying:

> Then you will call on Me and you will come and pray to Me, and I will hear [your voice] *and* I will listen to you. Then [with a deep longing] you will seek Me *and* require Me [as a vital necessity] and [you will] find Me when you search for Me with all your heart.

Jeremiah 29:12-13 (AMP)

God just wants a sincere, genuine heart coming to Him, acknowledging who He is and that He is the answer to everything.

Prayer is so powerful that the devil tries to trip us up by praying the wrong way. He wants us to get sidetracked from what we are supposed to be doing, and that is simply talking to God and listening to what God has to say. The Bible gives us examples of how we ought to pray.

> Also, when you pray, do not be like the hypocrites; for they love to pray [publicly] standing in the synagogues and on the corners of the streets so that they may be seen by men. I assure you *and* most solemnly say to you, they [already] have their reward in full.

But when you pray, go into your most private room, close the door and pray to your Father who is in secret, and your Father who sees [what is done] in secret will reward you. "And when you pray, do not use meaningless repetition as the Gentiles do, for they think they will be heard because of their many words. So, do not be like them [praying as they do]; for your Father knows what you need before you ask Him. "Pray, then, in this way: 'Our Father, who is in heaven, Hallowed be Your name. Your kingdom come, Your will be done On earth as it is in heaven. Give us this day our daily bread. And forgive us our debts, as we have forgiven our debtors [letting go of both the wrong and the resentment]. And do not lead us into temptation but deliver us from evil. [For Yours is the kingdom and the power and the glory forever. Amen.]' For if you forgive others their trespasses [their reckless and willful sins], your heavenly Father will also forgive you. But if you do not forgive others [nurturing your hurt and anger with the result that it interferes with your relationship with God], then your Father will not forgive your trespasses.

Matthew 6:5-15 (AMP)

The devil wants us to allow the BS to be on exhibit when we pray. The Bible plainly says, "do not pray like hypocrites, phonies, and pretenders." God knows everything, even the thoughts before we think them, so there is no need to try to put on with Him or be fake. When the Word said do not be like the hypocrites; for they love to pray publicly standing in the synagogues and on the corners of the streets so that they may be seen by men. Haven't you seen or know people that will pray when they are in church before people, or we like to say when they have the microphone, and the spotlight is on them, you can't get them to stop praying! But when they are at home, or it is just a few people in the church that day, they pray short or without the same fervent passion because there is no crowd. I have heard comedians and other people make jokes about the prayers of some of the deacons in churches that they knew exactly what the deacons would say. The kids would mock them word for word, saying repetitious words. You would think that someone would have told them to hit the refresh prayer button. There is so much to pray about besides our four and no more. We have our families, friends, churches, schools, our cities, states, government, armed services, our nations, and the world and the list goes on. This is a broad spectrum because crime is inside our cities, states, nations, and sickness and disease are at an all-time high. We see the signs of the end times are upon us, and that means time is wrapping up. If there has ever been a time to pray, it is now! We need the God of the Bible like never before. We need God's protection, God's direction, God's anointing, and God's power, the Holy Spirit. There is so much more that I can list that we need, but I believe you get the point.

Some Things Are Just Private

There are many ways to pray. One way is private prayers. Private prayer time is between you and God, we should consider private prayer like we handle other people, this is nobody's business. Our private personal time with God is so special and gratifying and fulfilling. This is a time that you can be free. Free to talk to your Heavenly Father about anything and everything. You can unload because God is never overloaded or have too much to handle. There is nothing that we can say or experience that can make God ponder or wonder if He can handle it. There is nothing in this world or out of this world that God cannot handle. God is the creator of all things. Isaiah 59:1 (EXB) tells us: "Surely the LORD's power [hand] is enough [not too short] to save you. He can hear you when you ask him for help [...nor his ear too heavy to hear]."

Even in our private prayer time, sometimes we do not know what to pray. Jesus has given us a format to pray from Matthew 6:9-13. This prayer covers everything, so what I do is pray this prayer every day in conjunction with my daily prayers making sure I cover every area of my life.

The Word let us know that God hears us when we pray. It does not matter if the prayer request is simple or urgent God can answer. Jeremiah 32:17 (ESV) says: "Ah, Lord God! It is you who have made the heavens and the earth by your great power and by your outstretched arm! Nothing is too hard for you."

Our God, our Father, is the Creator of all things. Everything was made by God, even the devil. Knowing this lets me know that nothing I can face, have, or experience is too hard for God! We serve a *mighty God*!

What a sweet personal, and transparent time this is to spend with our heavenly Father with no reservation. Thank you, Father, for giving us private one on one prayer time with You. We love You. ~

~ Die to Live...~

Results of Prayer

There are so many examples of the results of prayer. The first person that comes to my mind is Daniel. Daniel was known for praying. His praying got him into so much trouble, but his praying also got him out of it all. I admire Daniel for his faith, commitment, trust, and his adamant and obdurate belief in his God. Daniel would not yield no matter what! I have not read where his faith or trust wavered. What an amazing belief he had in God that it did not matter what the situation he was put in he knew his God could bring him out. Daniel was in the Old Testament, which means that the Holy Spirit had not come to dwell inside the believer because Jesus had not been born to Mary and died on the cross. I often wonder why it is a struggle for we as saints of God that say we have the Holy Spirit in our souls, and we faint or doubt sometimes. How could this be? I believe the BS, the beastly spirit is our number one enemy! Our flesh! Our fleshly sinful nature, the beast that lies within us makes me speechless…

Friends, we got to get to the point like Daniel that no matter what it is, or what it looks like, or what we might be told, we must know beyond a shadow of a doubt that God is able! Luke 1:37 (AMP) says: "For with God nothing [is or ever] shall be impossible."

Do you believe it?

We serve a God that cannot lie. God is the same yesterday, today, and forevermore! Rest assured that God will perform His Word Jeremiah 1:12 (AMPC) says: "Then said the Lord to me, You have seen well, for I am alert *and* active, watching over My word to perform it."

The eyes of the Lord are everywhere, and God is watching to see who is praying, speaking, living, and believing His Word so He can perform it. Why pray if you do not believe God's

Word?

> And it is impossible to please God without faith. Anyone who wants to come to him must believe that God exists and that he rewards those who sincerely seek him.
>
> Hebrews 11:6 (NLT)

Faith is the key component to prayer; without faith, we just have empty words.

Do You Have a Testimony?

I would like to believe that everyone reading this book has a testimony or something that they know God has done for them. I have so many testimonies that I cannot count them all, but even so, when I came up against insurmountable situations in my life, the BS would be right there, and I would find myself praying and giving the situation to God but worry. If worry was there, that meant doubt was there too. I thank God that as life went on, I was able through the Holy Spirit to defeat the beast more than not when it came to overwhelming situations.

A couple of testimonies I witnessed. One Sunday, a lady visited our church. She had stage four cancer. She asked for prayer for healing. She came to the alter, and our pastor prayed for her and asked me to lay my hands on her since I have the gift of healing. A couple of weeks later, she came back to the church, rejoicing that she went to her doctor and they took several tests on her and they could not find any cancer in her body! Our pastor told her that it was wonderful that she was healed, but her soul was still sick and that she needed to accept Jesus as her Savior. Sadly to say, she did not. Later we found out she went to Las Vegas and partied like a rock star, and we never saw her again.

Another testimony from the results of prayer is from a prayer cloth that was given to an eight-year-old boy who lost his sight in one of his eyes due to a car accident. One day, one of the members at the church worked in the eye clinic. The optometrist had told the boy's mom that they would have to do surgery on his eye to get the glass out, but he would not be able to see out of it. So, the member told his mom that God could work a miracle for her son if she believed. She told her that she seen miracles performed at our church. She gave the boy's mom one of the purple prayer cloth and told her to put it on the boy's eye and believe when she prays for him that he would get his sight back. The lady was receptive and did as she was instructed.

You might be wondering what the meaning of the prayer cloth is. Our pastor took the example from Acts 19:11-12 (AMP) where it says:

> God was doing extraordinary *and* unusual miracles by the hands of Paul, so that even handkerchiefs *or* face-towels or aprons that had touched his skin were brought to the sick, and their diseases left them and the evil spirits came out [of them].
>
> Acts 19:11-12 (AMP)

The prayer cloth came from a forty-day consecration where our pastor fasted and gave God a tenth of the fast by staying in the church, wrapping himself up in a large piece of purple cloth for four days laying on the altar. The only time he left the altar was to use the restroom. After the consecration was over, the cloth was cut into squares and given out to people that needed healing.

Now back to the testimony, about a week later, we were having a city-wide back to school prayer, and the boy and his mom came to the church and testified that the child was scheduled for surgery, and after receiving the prayer cloth, she prayed for her son and when he went back to the doctor they performed an exam and found out that the child could see and the glass was gone! To God be the glory!

One more testimony is that our pastor, my husband, was told he had cancer in the bladder. He did not tell anyone but me and asked me to pray with him. He was bleeding, having to use medical pads the doctor gave him to absorb the blood. We both continued as usual in life doing ministry trusting and believing God to do the miraculous. One day we were heading to Thursday intercessory prayer at the church. It was about 7:25 p.m. when his doctor called him after hours. My husband answered the phone. His doctor told him that he had to send his lab work off to a specialist to make sure that the test result was accurate. The test came back with *no trace of cancer*! *God did it again*! All praises go to our magnificent God!

Attach Fasting to Prayer

But when you fast, put oil on your head [as you normally would to groom your hair] and wash your face so that your fasting will not be noticed by people, but by your Father who is in secret; and your Father who sees [what is done] in secret will reward you.

Matthew 6:17-18 (AMP)

The word (when) also can be used by saying whenever or as. Reading Matthew 6:17 using either of those words, it would read as: But whenever you fast, or as you fast. The word when tells us that this is something that we must do. It is not an option, it is a doing. Fasting is relevant and pertinent to our prayer life. My pastor always says, "You can pray without fasting, but you cannot fast without praying." Fasting and praying go hand and hand.

Fasting is an area that the BS, the beastly spirit, our flesh fights us because the flesh does not want to die. Fasting is another key element to our prayer life. When we attach fasting to prayer, we have a mighty force on our side. I told God I wanted to live like I fast! What I mean by this is that I want to live the way I lived while I was on the fast. I want the fasting lifestyle to become a part of my daily routine.

When I am fasting, my life, my whole day is different. It is like I am existing in another world yet living in this one. I wake up praying, I pray all the way to work and back home. I listen to the Word of God by a preacher or just letting the Bible read back to me. On my lunch and break, I am praying and reading the Word. My day is filled with God, and what a difference of a day that makes. Things in the world do not grab my attention, and my mind is free to receive more godly thoughts. Interacting with people is different as well, my discernment intensity is on a hundred! How can I put this? It is like I can see through them or the spirit that is attached to them that may make them say or act a certain way. Because the Holy Spirit is in full control, He gives me the advantage to defeat the enemy's shots. He tries to shoot through them, trying to get me to mess up my day or the fast.

My mind stays on Jesus, so therefore peace is there. Things that come up do not rattle me like it would when my soul is full of God and the Holy Spirit. I am not saying we should live all day in heaven. There must be a balance in life. I believe a balanced life is different for each individual because everyone is not at the same place in God. For instance, if someone is a babe in Christ or a new believer, they need to eat more of the things of God than someone that has been in the walk of salvation for years. Since we need balance in our lives, why not ask the Holy Spirit to be our scale? Why not put our everyday living on the scale of life and allow the Holy Spirit to tilt and balance the scale to whichever side we are giving the most of ourselves to? Then we can balance out our lives to please God.

Some Things Only Come out by Prayer and Fasting

Matthew 17:19-21(EXB) says:

> The followers [disciples] came to Jesus when he was alone and asked, "Why couldn't we force [drive; cast] the demon out?" Jesus answered, "Because your faith is too small [you have so little faith]. I tell you the truth, if your faith is as big as [as small as; the size of; as; like] a mustard seed, you can say to this mountain, Move from here to there, and it will move. All things will be possible [Nothing would be impossible] for you. That kind of spirit comes out only if you use prayer and fasting."

> Matthew 17:19-21(EXB)

Have you ever been suppressed in your spirit or just could not shake off a mood or attitude? Your thoughts just could not be freed from stinking thinking and the negativity of life? I am not saying that you have a demon inside of you, but sometimes we are oppressed and tormented by evil spirits. Sometimes we are overloaded with a situation that we just can't get any release, whether it's sickness, a wayward child, spiritual blockage, lack of finance, etc.. For us to get a breakthrough, we have to add fasting to our prayer with faith and watch God move.

God will perform His Word. Even when you receive your answer to your prayer request, do not stop praying. Continue living each day like you were still on a fast. I believe this is one of our secret weapons against the enemy and our flesh.

Keep the secret weapon of fasting and prayer sharpened. When you were fasting, and you found yourself reading the Bible more, continue doing that. If you prayed more, continue praying. If you found yourself praising God more or meditating on the Word or the things of God, do not stop. Keep living the Word, speak it, confess it, hold on to it, hide it in your hearts, and include praise and worship. If we continue living like we are fasting, our hearts, minds, and souls will continue in a sanctification state of being sanctified, which simply means being set apart of God's use and the BS the beastly spirit will be crucified day by day!

Can you see why the devil does not want us to fast or pray? Look at all the benefits that come with praying and fasting. The devil knows the power of God, so he will try anything to keep us bogged down and depressed, disappointed, in despair, full of doubt and fears to keep us from the source of everything, which is God!

Fasting and Prayer Will Sanctify Us

Therefore I urge you, brothers and sisters, by the mercies of God, to present your bodies [dedicating all of yourselves, set apart] as a living sacrifice, holy and well-pleasing to God, *which is* your rational (logical, intelligent) act of worship. And do not be conformed to this world [any longer with its superficial values and customs], but be transformed *and* progressively changed [as you mature spiritually] by the renewing of your mind [focusing on godly values and ethical attitudes], so that you may prove [for yourselves] what the will of God is, that which is good and acceptable and perfect [in His plan and purpose for you].

Romans 12:1-2 (AMP)

Paul is begging us to live a sanctified set apart holy life that would please God. Praying and fasting will help us in the sanctifying process. I believe this is one of the reasons the Bible tells us to pray without ceasing. God does not want us to live, think, and act like the world. By praying and fasting and yielding to God's Word and His will our minds will be in a progressively increasingly transforming state. God wants us to be separated from the BS, the flesh, so we will be acceptable and perfect for His plan and purpose that He has for us.

"Even now," says the LORD, "Turn and come to Me with all your heart [in genuine repentance], With fasting and weeping and mourning [until every barrier is removed and the broken fellowship is restored]; Rip your heart to pieces [in sorrow and contrition] and not your garments." Now return [in repentance] to the LORD *your God*, For He is gracious and compassionate, slow to anger, abounding in lovingkindness [faithful to His covenant with His people]; And He relents [His sentence of] evil [when His people genuinely repent].

Joel 2:12-13 (AMP)

~ Die to Live...~

Testimony of God's Miraculous Power

We need faith, prayer, and fasting to get our desired results. Unfortunately, some people do not believe in the power of prayer this is incredibly sad because I know for a fact prayer works! I have so many testimonies of the results of prayer that I cannot name them all. I am thankful God always hears us, how amazing to know that God is never too busy or tired from this chaotic world to hear or help us. Thank you, Lord!

Testimony

Whenever my husband and I get the opportunity, we share this testimony of God's miraculous power. We had been married for eleven years with no pregnancy, and God told my husband if we would move to Kentucky and start a church that He would give us a child. We had been working in the ministry for over two years. We were working so hard that we did not have time to dwell on a child. As time when on, I missed my cycle, and I ignored it because I had so many false alarms that I did not want to take another pregnancy test, and the test came back negative again. So, I finally got up enough nerves to take a home pregnancy test. I did not tell my husband because I did not want to get him all excited. I took the test, and to my surprise, it came back positive! *Wow*! I could not wait to tell my husband the good news! I called him at work and asked him to meet me for lunch. When I told him this exciting great news, he was overjoyed! I begged him not to tell his mother or my mother until I went to my doctor to confirm the test results. I made an appointment for the next day, and sure enough, I was pregnant! We were so excited and could not wait to tell our family and friends! As time went on and we continued working in the church and working on our jobs. At every doctor's appointment, my husband was there with me. Would you believe that I had over eleven ultrasounds, and they could not tell if the baby was a boy or girl? My husband said boldly, "I know for a fact it is a boy because that is what God told me." I also had asked God for a male child. When people would ask what we should buy the baby, my husband would say, "Boy clothing, boy toys, etc." He had an assurance and trust in God, he knows God to be a promise keeper.

One day I was in the kitchen cooking dinner and felt water running down my legs. I went to the bathroom, and it was pouring out. I called my husband downstairs and told him what was going on, and he said we need to call the doctor. I called the doctor, and the doctor said to go to the hospital emergency room as soon as possible because it sounds like your water had burst. I was stunned. When we arrived at the hospital, I was rush back, and the doctors begin testing immediately because I was only about twenty-two weeks gestation. I was given a choice to have the child or let it die because the doctor said if I had him, he was going to be retarded, blind, deaf, cerebral posy, the bottom line if I had the child, he would be in a vegetative state of being and this was just some of the things the doctor said the baby would have. The doctor left the room so we could discuss rather or not to have the child or miscarry. We both said we are trusting God no matter what and that we would love the baby no matter what the outcome would be.

I was placed in a room where I was monitored uninterrupted. I was placed in a bed that kept my legs elevated up in hopes that the baby would not come. After about a week, the doctors said they thought it was okay for them to put me in a regular room, and they would continue to watch me closely.

My husband stayed with me day and night. He most definitely gets the great husband award of the year! This whole situation is a miracle from the time of conception to the delivery.

On August 28th, about 8:40 a.m., my husband said he was going home to take a shower and change clothes. As soon as he got home at 9:04 a.m., the nurse called him to tell him

I had the baby! He felt horrible that he had left. But God is so amazing. He had orchestrated this miracle. There was a seasoned nurse on duty who was normally off that day which just so happened to be working. She told the other nurse to put me on my hands and knees, and they both put their hands against the area of my body, using their hands as a blockage, not allowing the baby to come out. That nurse was God sent! She told me later that she thanked God that she was there because this method was done many years ago and no longer performed. She said the newer nurses would not have had the knowledge to quickly assess the situation. She said if she had not performed this method, the baby would have died. To God be the glory for having that nurse in place at the right time.

Surgery

I remember the nurses running down the hall rushing me to surgery! There was no time to call my doctor, it just so happened an obstetrician was in the room! God had everything in place! The obstetrician performed an emergency C-section, and I delivered, at twenty-five-week gestation, one-pound-five-ounces, eleven-inch-long baby boy! Everything took about four minutes!

About the time my husband arrived at the hospital, he had missed it all. He could not believe it, but he was thankful the baby was alive. When he came into the room, he was crying. I did not know what had happened. I thought *he was going to tell me the baby did not make it*, but what he said was, "We have a beautiful baby *boy*." God is so good! We were so thankful! We thanked God for what He had done.

I was in and out because of the medication, but I could hear my husband saying our son was so small that his wedding ring could slide up and down his arms. This was the beginning of a one hundred fourteenth day's journey at the NIC unit of the University of Kentucky Hospital.

God Keeps His Promises

Jeremiah 33:3 (KJV): "Call unto me, and I will answer thee, and shew thee great and mighty things, which thou knowest not."

After five days, the doctor released me to go home. My mother came from Florida to be with me. I was so thankful; we had no family here with us. We have a small taste of what Abraham and Sarah felt like when they had to leave their kindred and go to a place they knew nothing of. We had a young church that only been in existence for a little over two years. God blessed us with some true saints that loved us. The day came that I was discharged. One of the elders from the church came to the hospital to pick up my mother and me and take us home. I will never forget that day as we drove off, leaving my little tiny miracle baby in the hospital, fighting for every breath he took. I did not get to hold him or touch him. Riding home was a blur as I felt warm little tears shaped like hearts roll down my cheeks. My husband stayed there with him praying and singing the "Yes Lord" song. Every time my husband would dose off and fall asleep, my son's lungs and heart rate would drop so low that the monitors would go off. The nurse came over to him and said, "Sir, whatever you are doing, don't stop because when you sing and pray, the baby's breathing stayed at 100 percent with the oxygen.

When we drove up to my house, I needed the strength of God to walk. I did not care about my physical condition, I just wanted my baby. This was not how we planned the coming home party to be. There were no balloons or welcome party of family and friends. Just complete silence. I felt as if I was going to faint. Right then, I knew God was with me as I felt the strength of God stand up inside of me.

My mother walked alongside me as I felt the warmth of her tender love. It seemed like nothing around was moving.

I heard no noise, just silence. It was as if I was walking on a cloud as I entered the door. Each step up the stairs felt like I was carrying a ton of bricks. I finally made it to my bedroom. I laid down and quietly prayed a small prayer asking God for His mercy and grace to be upon my son and let him live. I told God if He let my son live, I would give him back to Him just as Hannah did with her first son Samuel, which means "I have asked for him from the Lord" (1 Samuel 1:20, NKJV).

Ultimate Decision—Death Sentence

On September 6th, the doctor called me, my husband, and my mom in for a consultation to let us know that we had one choice to make in order for our son to live. We were told that the blood from his heart was leaking into his lungs, flooding the lungs, which would kill him. The doctor said they could perform surgery to try to stop the bleeding, but we had to sign the release papers, and there was only one side effect that could happen, and that was *death*. The doctor also said with all seriousness in his voice that with all the medical problems that our son has, if we loved our son, we should pull the plug and let the baby die because he would live a vegetative life. The doctor then turned to me and said, "You will be able to hold him for the first and last time for thirty minutes, then he will expire." Time stopped all around me. Where did everybody go? I felt as if I was all alone, even though all of them were sitting right there. My mind could not think, so I had to rely on my heart, and with a whispered voice, I said, "I leave this decision up to my husband, and whatever he says, that is what I will go with." The doctor said okay and asked who we would like to call to help us through this solemn time? He said we have a chaplain on duty, or "if you like, you can go to our chapel on the first floor." My mother looked at the doctor with boldness on her face and said, "We are calling in *Jesus!*" what we need to be done only our God can do. My husband said God promised us a child, and he was not going to let the devil get the victory. He said, "We will not pull the plug. My trust is in my God!"

When we signed the papers for the surgery in faith and trust in God, there was no time for a dot of doubt because this was a matter of life and death. The doctors made it clear to us that the surgery may not be successful, and there was only one side effect, and that was death. That night was crucial the doctor said it would be a miracle if my son makes it throughout the night. My son made it!

We saw the spirit of death in the NIC unit. We could see the sadness in the smiles of the parents. We were not only praying for our son, we were praying for all the other babies and their parents as well. It was about six babies that had died. When a baby died, the doctors would ask everyone to leave the room to let only the parents stay and have private time with their baby, and they would get time to spend those precious moments together for the last time. I never will forget there was a young couple about twenty years old. They were given the same speech that we were given. We prayed with them and told them that if they believed God, God could do anything. Sadly, to say they could not believe it, and their baby passed. We saw scriptures taped on some of the incubators of some of the babies. Not only death was in the room faith was there too. This whole event was new to us. We had never been in a NIC unit or been around premature babies. God opened our eyes to a world of prematurity that someone is experiencing every day, and so many people like us had no idea what goes on in this prematurity world.

The nurses told us that some of the parents could not handle seeing their child like this, so they would leave them there and never come back again. The nurses also said that some mothers that had a premature baby after they delivered the baby, that was it for them, they never went to see the baby. The babies that were left abandoned were awarded to the state to decide what the outcome would be.

Life Day!

September 6th is our son's life day! He celebrates August 28th as his birthday and September 6th as life day. During this week, we were so absorbed with our son's situation that everything else around us was put on hold until 911 hit! My mom was scheduled to fly back home to Florida that day. When we arrived at the airport, it was somewhat chaotic. People were everywhere, we went inside the airport, and everyone was standing in front of the television watching the breaking news that there were a series of four coordinated terrorist attacks by the Islamic terrorist group al-Qaeda against the United States on the morning of Tuesday, September 11th, 2001. The attacks killed 2,996 people, injured over 6,000 others, and caused at least $10 billion in infrastructure and property damage.

Our prayer alarm went off! We hit the 911 emergency button, which is *Jesus!* We immediately stopped focusing and praying for our son and began to pray for this horrific event! What a catastrophe this was. We saw people crying and calling on Jesus. Nobody was trying to be politically correct that day! No one said, "You can't say the name Jesus," it so amazing that when tragedy hits, Jesus is the first name people say.

"God is our refuge and strength, a very present help in trouble" (Psalm 46:1, KJV).

I am so thankful God is omnipresent. We all can be assured that no matter what is going on in this world, God is there. God's power never runs low or run out. God has enough power to help everyone in this whole world at the same time if He chooses to. God is sovereign. He answers to no one. He is

God, and there is none else.

Many years later, while in a mid-night cry prayer with my husband and our godmother, God we were praying and giving Him glory and praise for our son's life God spoke to me and said, "When you and your husband signed those papers, the doctors saw your names, but in the supernatural where death was fighting with life the death angels saw another signature." They saw the name of *Jesus* and the powerful healing name of *Jesus* canceled out death! And the surgery was a success! All glory goes to *God!* Hallelujah!

Persisted in Faith

The journey continued with my son. He ended up having heart surgery because blood was leaking into his lungs. The surgery was a success, all glory goes to God. He went through numerous tests. He had a category four bleed on the left hemisphere of his brain and category two on the right hemisphere of his brain. The doctors said they could put a rod in his brain to drain the blood out, but because of the persistency in faith and prayer, we asked God the heal his brain, and He did! The blood self-absorbed itself! I know God is real and can do anything, and that is not all! My son, during those 114 days, coded out several times, setting off the death alarms, but God brought him back each time! This saga of my son was a testing time for things to come for myself and my husband. When he left the hospital, the head doctor for the NIC unit said, "Your God is real. This child has beaten all the odds to God be the glory for what He has done!" I praise You, Lord, from the depths of my soul!

Stay Connected

I knew I had to stay cemented and glued to the Word of God constantly. As soon as I would let up, the devil was waiting to hammer my mind! The fight with the BS was a battle! Then I remembered that the battle is not mine, it is the Lord! Thank you, Jesus, that you are victorious in every battle! It is a fight for peace when we are facing uncontrollable situations, but we can obtain impeccable peace if we trust God. I had to have confident faith, knowing that God was able to heal and bless my son. I repeated throughout the day Jeremiah 32:17 (NKJV): "Behold, I am the LORD, the God of all flesh: is there anything too hard for me?"

I had to be committed and focus like never before; it was a matter of life and death for my child. I could not let family or friends, nobody no one break the chains of faith and trust in God. My faith had to be solid. If I can do it, you can too! The more I trusted God the more love flooded my heart, casting out all fear. God is a reward to those who seek him. Hebrews 11:6 (GWT) says: "No one can please God without faith. Whoever goes to God must believe that God exists and that he rewards those who seek him."

I cannot tell you that it was easy because it was not. Each day holds its own struggle. One day we would go to see my baby, the doctors said he is doing good, the next day we would hear, "Oh, I am sorry things are not looking good prepare yourself." This was on and off for, like I said, "One hundred fourteen days," but I knew doubt could not be found in your heart, mind, or soul. It must be 100 percent faith and trust that God is able and believe me, friends God is able!

Whatever you do keep your mind stayed on Jesus, and He will keep you in peace I am a witness.

~Die to Live...~

Be Encouraged

Dear reader, if you are a mother, a parent that is experiencing life with a child born premature and you have received devastating reports, I want you to be encouraged because God has the last say on everything. Whatever you are facing, please know you are not alone. The enemy wants us to think that God is not with us or God does not care; that is a lie. God cares. He even tells us in 1 Peter 5:7 (AMP) to cast all your cares [all your anxieties, all your worries, and all your concerns, once and for all] on Him, for He cares about you [with deepest affection, and watches over you very carefully].

I could not have made it through without casting all my fears, worries, and concerns on God. When the enemy tried to bombard my mind with negative thoughts or I would hear what the doctors would say over and over in my mind what the outcome was going to be, I would go to the Word of God and pray the scriptures out loud. I would go to Isaiah 26:3-4 (AMP):

> You will keep in perfect *and* constant peace *the one* whose mind is steadfast [that is, committed and focused on You—in both inclination and character], Because he trusts *and* takes refuge in You [with hope and confident expectation]. "Trust [confidently] in the LORD forever [He is your fortress, your shield, your banner], For the LORD GOD is an everlasting Rock [the Rock of Ages].

> Isaiah 26:3-4 (AMP

The Miraculous Power of God

Our son is truly a miracle. The miraculous power of God has prevailed all throughout his life. Our son was in the graduating class of 2020. He made the honor roll his eleventh and twelfth-grade year! This is amazing when I think about it because the doctors said he would never be able to see more, less read and learn. He was homecoming king, and he was able to give the miraculous testimony of what God had done in his life at his baccalaureate ceremony! God is utterly incredible and deserves all the glory and praise! Just Believe!

Never Stop Praying

First Thessalonians 5:17 (KJV): "Pray without ceasing."

The bottom-line prayer works! We had the two and three gathered in Jesus's name, praying! Not only we were praying, but family and friends and the body of Christ throughout had locked in with us in prayer. Father, thank you for the power of prayer and faith!

Prayer is what has kept my mind held together from the traumas of life. I have called on God so many times that I know God knows me! This whole book is wrapped up in prayer. All the experiences and situations prayer were there in them all. I heard people say, "God does not answer prayer." My question is why there would be so many scriptures in the Bible that tells us about prayer and that we need to do it. One scripture that immediately comes to my mind is 1 Thessalonians 5:17 (NLT): "Never stop praying."

Never means never. We do not get an excuse card not to pray. We must talk to God. If you are saved by accepting Jesus as Savior, then you no longer belong to yourself, you belong to God. Jesus paid a great price for us to be able to simply talk (pray) to God. The price was so great that it cost Him His life! Our Father loves us unconditionally, absolutely, and completely. Let us love Him back and communicate with our Father. Colossians 4:2 (AMP) says: "Be persistent *and* devoted to prayer, being alert *and* focused in your prayer life with *an attitude of* thanksgiving."

We can do this! You got this! Let us pray and see what the end is going to be. Blessings!

Pray in the Will of God

> For this reason I am telling you, whatever things you ask for in prayer [in accordance with God's will], believe [with confident trust] that you have received them, and they will be *given* to you.

> Mark 11:24 (AMP)

Praying according to God's will believing with great confidence is always the best way to pray. When I pray, I ask God to show me His will, I want to identify and recognize His will like I see the sky, there is no doubt when I see the sky, I know it is the sky. I do not want to error. I want to pray God's Word back to Him because Isaiah 55:11 (AMP) says:

> So will My word be which goes out of My mouth; It will not return to Me void (useless, without result), Without accomplishing what I desire, And without succeeding *in the matter* for which I sent it.

Listen to what Isaiah is saying, "If we want the assurance to our prayer request then it behooves us to pray the Word of God. God will perform His Word, it will not return to Him without results." I once heard this scripture put like this the

Word cannot go back to God until it does what it was sent out to do, what a wonderful assurance that is. Jesus even told us in Matthew 4:4 (AMP):

> But Jesus replied, "It is written *and* forever remains written, 'MAN SHALL NOT LIVE BY BREAD ALONE, BUT BY EVERY WORD THAT COMES OUT OF THE MOUTH OF GOD.'"

If we want a guarantee that our prayers will be answered, then pray the Word of God back to God. I don't want to pray for anything that is not in the Will of God, what would it profit me to get what I am asking for when it is all null and void and useless to God? Why would we want stale fruit which is (our will), when we can have fresh fruit, God's will? God gives us the best when it is in His will.

I know what it is like to pray out of the Will of God. I remember praying in my twenties for this sport's car. Boy, did I want that car! I kept asking God, and when I did not hear from Him or get the green light, I made my own decision, and I ignored the fact that it was not God's will. So, guess what I did? I bought the car anyway! What a mistake that was, I had trouble after trouble with that car. I finally had to admit I bought a lemon! I ended up having to put a supposedly new engine in the car later to find out that the repair shop had lied to me and put an old engine in the car! I ended up paying them thousands of dollars for my disobedience. I eventually had to take the auto repair shop to court. I ended up winning the case, but I never saw the money. This was all because I did not obey the will of God. That was truly a life lesson for me. I learned that after you pray, don't ignore the answer to your prayer; after all, we asked for it, we must accept God's will and God's way, and if we do, we will have guaranteed victory!

~Die to Live...~

Evelyn A. Johnson

Prayer Goes into the Unseen Future

The secret to prayer is that we do not know when the prayer request will be manifested in our lives. Imagine your prayers being stored in a prayer vault. The devil cannot get inside of your vault because only God has the combination, which is our faith. The size of your vault is determined by how much time you spend in prayer. Since we do not know what each day brings, we must always pray. One day you might need God for an unseen situation that has occurred in your life, and because you have stored prayers in your vault, God opens the vault and apply that prayer attached with the answer right then and there. For instance, you might have a prayer for protection from all hurt, harm, and danger in your vault. You may not have encountered a harmful event that day you prayed that prayer, but your prayer request was stored. Prayer is powerful and lasting.

Here is a testimony to a stored prayer:

Dedicated to the Assignment ~

One day my husband was on his way to pick up some pews that another church had given us. As he was driving, the light turned green, and an elderly lady ran the red light and crashed into him! She said she did not see the red light. This collision caused my husband to be in excruciating pain. He has a high pain tolerance, but it was getting to be unbearable. He was in so much pain that he would come to church but lay in two chairs pulled together, making a bed until it was time for him to preach. He was preaching, praying, playing the organ for worship, working on a job all in pain. He told the church that he looked forward to preaching and praying because the anointing of God would be on him, and during that time, the pain was gone, that was the only time he would get a release from the pain. He was so committed to pleasing God that he would not stop. He was committed to the commitment.

Even though he was committed, it did not stop the pain. The day came that he could not take the pain anymore and ended up having his first back surgery. I believe when there is a great call on your life, the enemy will try to stop you. The surgery went well, and we just knew he was on his way to recovery.

Days later, my husband said something is not right, "I should not still be in this much pain." Come to find out, there was a nurse on duty that did not wash her hands or put on gloves when he was in the hospital, because of her careless act, he ended up with a staph infection! The doctor sent him home with a pick line in his arm. He had to dispense the medication once a day. I turned into a nurse overnight. The surgery left a hole in his back that I had to change out the gauze, unpacking and repacking the hole daily. I had to be incredibly careful to keep everything sterile. I know for a fact that we can do all things through Jesus, who gives us the strength to do whatever we need to do and become whatever we need to be.

My husband was so committed to his assignment that he continued going to church. I recall the church had a "seven hours of power prayer" the prayer was announced on the radio every day leading up to that day. We begin receiving prayer requests from all over. The day came, and our pastor prayed for seven hours straight! He asked God to hold his bladder until the prayer was over, and God did! Great testimonies came from that prayer! All glory goes to God!

Unseen Prayer Receives Visible Results

Can you see prayer? We cannot see prayer or words coming out of our mouths but what we see is the *results*! A lot of times we pray, and the manifestations of our prayer are not visible to the natural eye, but in the spirit realm, the manifestation has occurred. I believe the scripture from Matthew 21:22 (EXB): "If you believe [have faith], you will get anything you ask for in prayer."

Nowhere in this verse does it say if you believe, you will get anything you ask for in prayer tomorrow, within a week, or on a certain day. The scripture says, "You will get what you ask for in prayer if you simply believe."

We must believe and not doubt and rely on God's perfect timing for the manifestation of the prayer request to take place. I believe the key to faith is believing until it happens.

Too many times we pray, and we do believe, but when the answer is not manifested within the time frame we thought it should have, we begin to doubt. We talk, worry, doubt ourselves right out of the victory. We start trying to figure it out or try to figure out how God is going to answer our prayer. We look for the answers in the wrong places. We look for family and friends to tell us something, we look for a sign, anything, than to just wait on God. We all have heard the saying, "Why pray if you are going to doubt?" What is the logic to that? It almost like we are praying, "Father, I ask in Jesus's name for healing, but I know you cannot heal, but I ask anyway." Does that make sense? No!

But when you ask, you must believe and not doubt, because the one who doubts is like a wave of the sea, blown and tossed by the wind. That person should not expect to receive anything from the Lord. Such a person is double-minded and unstable in all they do.

James 1:6-8 (NIV)

We do not want to be unstable, erratic, and inconsistent in our faith. These actions will cause an immediate cancelation of our prayer request.

God just wants us to trust Him and know that He will always do what is best for us in every area of our lives. Stay in faith.

~ Die to Live...~

Prayer Helps You to Think Clearly

This is one of the main areas of the BS, the beastly spirit wants to be in control and that is the mind, as was stated in chapter two. Prayer is so amazing! I believe prayer helps us to think sensible and rationally. When we pray, we enter the supernatural causing the unseen world to be manifested in the natural.

Have you ever been in a situation and your mind was clouded with all kinds of thoughts? You did not know which decision to make, and you prayed, and God gave you clarity of thought, and you made the right decision. What a wonderful experience that is to receive a victorious outcome all because of prayer!

One way prayer helps me to think clearly is that I pray the Word of God back to God.

First Peter 4:7 (AMP) is a good scripture to pray back to God, it says:

> The end *and* culmination of all things is near. Therefore, be sound-minded and self-controlled for the purpose of prayer [staying balanced and focused on the things of God so that your communication will be clear, reasonable, specific, and pleasing to Him.]

1 Peter 4:7 (AMP)

When we pray, we want to ask for a sound mind, self-control, and to stay balanced and focused. This verse is saying we need to be clear and intentional about what we are praying for. A sound mind does not depend on human wisdom or human strength, a sound mind is not controlled by the flesh. God will give us through His Spirit a sound mind.

We need to be reasonable, realistic, and specific so we will please God. We do not impress God when we pray lofty prayers. We must be intentional purposeful in what we are praying for. We need to have self-control to be able to stay focused and not pray about any and everything but be centered in our thoughts. I have heard people praying for healing and jumped into praying for a dog or a cat. No connection was made. No focus, the attention span has gone! We should not have ADHD in prayer.

When we pray, ask God to take our mind and transform it, renew it because we do not want the fleshly mind that opposes God to be in control.

I remember one night, the leadership in our church was fasting and praying for our pastor, who was preparing himself to enter into a forty-day fast with no food. I prayed and asked God to feed him manna from heaven. Not food, but let the manna be the Word of God. I asked God to feed him with all the knowledge of His will so that when he comes out of the consecration, he will be so filled with the Word of God that his counter-ness change and the anointing of God would glow on him that lives would be transformed for God's glory! I prayed and asked God to strengthen the natural body so that it would be able to house or hold the Holy Spirit. God answered the prayer, and the mountain of the BS, the will of the flesh, was thrown into the sea, and our pastor completed the forty days of fasting and prayer with a victorious outcome!

> And Jesus answered them, "Have faith in God. Truly, I say to you, whoever says to this mountain, 'Be taken up and thrown into the sea,'

and does not doubt in his heart, but believes that what he says will come to pass, it will be done for him. Therefore I tell you, whatever you ask in prayer, believe that you have received it, and it will be yours.

Mark 11:22-24

I End This Chapter with a Prayer for New Clay ~

"Yet you, LORD, are our Father. We are the clay; you are the potter; we are all the work of your hand" (Isaiah 64:8, NIV)

Father, Your Word says you are the Potter, and we are the clay. I pray that you take our clay bodies and mold, make, shape, and re-make us again. Remake us just like when we play with playdough, we take that dough and tear it apart and build and rebuild until we get it to look like the image we had in our mind.

Father, when you created human beings, you created them in your image. I pray that you take our clay head, the old way of thinking, and replace it with the mind of Christ. Take out our old dull, spiritually blinded eyes and put in the bright light eyes of Christ so that we would see as Jesus sees. We want to have a perspective like Jesus in every area of our lives. Take our clay mouth and give us a new mouth. A mouth that would speak words of wisdom and love and never negativity. Take our clay ears and give us new ears to hear what your Holy Spirit tells us in the name of Jesus. Block out the voices of our enemy, the devil, and the flesh. Take out our clay hearts that have stones in them and give us a pure heart like Christ. Give us the heart of Jesus that is full of love and mercy for everyone, everybody, every human being! Father, if any part of our bodies is sick or in pain, replace that limb with a new part because You are able! If they have weak legs, give them new clay legs with the strength of God in them, so they can walk and do your will. If they have bad feet, give them new clay feet that their feet will take them wherever You want them to go. If their hands are in pain, give them new clay hands that their hands would be blessed and be able to help one another. If they have weak or painful arms, give them new clay arms to carry the loads of life in the power of the Holy Spirit. Father, thank you for being the creator of all things, especially mankind. We love You, and we pray this prayer in Jesus's name. Amen.

~ *Die to Live…* ~

Powerful Prayer Scriptures

Luke 18:1 (AMP): "Now Jesus was telling the disciples a parable to make the point that at all times they ought to pray and not give up *and* lose heart."

Mark 11:24 (KJV): "Therefore I say unto you, What things soever ye desire, when ye pray, believe that ye receive them, and ye shall have them."

First John 5:14 (KJV): "And this is the confidence that we have in him, that, if we ask any thing according to his will, he heareth us."

John 15:7 (KJV): "If ye abide in me, and my words abide in you, ye shall ask what ye will, and it shall be done unto you."

Matthew 7:7 (KJV): "Ask, and it shall be given you; seek, and ye shall find; knock, and it shall be opened unto you."

> Ye have not chosen me, but I have chosen
> you, and ordained you, that ye should go and
> bring forth fruit, and [that] your fruit should re-
> main: that whatsoever ye shall ask of the Father
> in my name, he may give it you.
>
> John 15:16 (KJV)

Isaiah 65:24 (KJV): "And it shall come to pass, that before they call, I will answer; and while they are yet speaking, I will hear."

First John 3:22 (KJV): "And whatsoever we ask, we receive of him, because we keep his commandments, and do those things that are pleasing in his sight."

Psalm 37:4 (KJV): "Delight thyself also in the Lord; and he shall give thee the desires of thine heart."

James 5:16 (KJV): "Confess your faults one to another,

and pray one for another, that ye may be healed. The effectual fervent prayer of a righteous man availeth much."

> If my people, which are called by my name, shall humble themselves, and pray, and seek my face, and turn from their wicked ways; then will I hear from heaven, and will forgive their sin, and will heal their land.

> 2 Chronicles 7:14 (KJV)

Jeremiah 29:12 (KJV): "Then shall ye call upon me, and ye shall go and pray unto me, and I will hearken unto you."

John 16:23 (KJV): "And in that day ye shall ask me nothing. Verily, verily, I say unto you, Whatsoever ye shall ask the Father in my name, he will give it you."

First John 1:9 (KJV): "If we confess our sins, he is faithful and just to forgive us our sins, and to cleanse us from all unrighteousness."

> Again I say unto you, That if two of you shall agree on earth as touching anything that they shall ask, it shall be done for them of my Father which is in heaven.

> Matthew 18:19 (KJV)

~ Die to Live... ~

The Beauty of Jesus Christ

~ Being beautiful inside make you radiant on the outside ~

But the Lord said to Samuel, "Don't look at·how handsome Eliab is [his appearance] or·how tall he is [his height], because I have ·not chosen [rejected] him. God does not see the same way [as] people see. People look at the outside of a person [appearances; the outward appearance], but the LORD looks at [on] the -heart.

1 Samuel 16:7 (EXB)

What is beauty? Beauty is not what is on the outside but, most importantly, what is on the inside...

First, I want to say I am so proud of you for getting almost to the end of *The Beastly Spirit—Dying to Live*. This book has been an incredible journey of the real fight of daily living as a Christian.

Jesus is "Beauty." Jesus is the radiance, illuminate the brilliant shining light that explodes from our souls!

I believe that true beauty is not how the world defines beauty, but it is the pureness of every heartbeat that would beat the love of Jesus Christ. Beauty is the pureness of the mind, soul, actions, attitudes, words, tones, perspective, and everyday living. When I think of beauty, I envision the magnificence splendor of Jesus the Christ. Not just His radiance of grace and mercy but the indescribable love that He has for all humanity.

Jesus is the Beauty

Our magnificence Savior Jesus the Christ is the beauty of *what* is the significance of a godly life, the *when* of eternity, the *why* of salvation, the *who* our Savior, and the *how* to have a victorious life on earth and forevermore.

Colossians 1:15-23 (AMP) gives us a glorious image of our Savior Jesus Christ. It reads:

> He is the exact living image [the essential manifestation] of the unseen God [the visible representation of the invisible], the firstborn [the preeminent one, the sovereign, and the originator] of all creation. For by Him all things were created in heaven and on earth, [things] visible and invisible, whether thrones or dominions or rulers or authorities; all things were created *and* exist through Him [that is, by His activity] and for Him. And He Himself existed *and* is before all things, and in Him all things hold together. [His is the controlling, cohesive force of the universe.] He is also the head [the life-source and leader] of the body, the church; and He is the beginning, the firstborn from the dead, so that He Himself will occupy the first place [He will stand supreme and be preeminent] in everything. For it pleased the *Father* for all the fullness [of deity—the sum total of His essence, all His perfection, powers, and attributes] to dwell [permanently] in Him (the Son), and through [the intervention of] the Son to reconcile all things to Himself, making peace [with believers] through the blood of His cross; through Him, [I say,] whether things on earth or things in heaven. And although you were at

one time estranged *and* alienated and hostile-minded [toward Him], *participating* in evil things, yet Christ has now reconciled you [to God] in His physical body through death, in order to present you before the Father holy and blameless and beyond reproach—[and He will do this] if you continue in the faith, well-grounded and steadfast, and not shifting away from the [confident] hope [that is a result] of the gospel that you have heard, which was proclaimed in all creation under heaven, and of which [gospel] I, Paul, was made a minister.

Colossians 1:15-23 (AMP)

Thank you, Jesus, for being the life source and the leader of our souls.

~ Die to Live...~

Jesus Is Love

Jesus is love that came down from heaven to earth. When our Father needed someone to redeem mankind, He asked His Son, who knew no sin to take on the ugly, horrible, nasty, dreadful, terrible, horrific stinking sin for me and you and the entire human race that we would become beautiful before our Creator, our Father. Jesus, He is the head of the body, which is the church. He is the beginning [meaning (1) the source of the church; (2) the creator of all things; or (3) the beginning/initiator of the end-time resurrection]. He is the first one who was raised [firstborn] from the dead. So in all things, Jesus has a first-place [supremacy] (Colossians 1:18, AMP).

I Want to Be Beautiful

Many nights as I was writing this book, tears would soak my dress because I wanted to be beautiful before my God. I would stop and pray, ask God for forgiveness, and help me because the beast in me, my flesh, was trying to control my thoughts and write! I said, "God, I did not want to write this book out of my flesh but from His Holy Spirit." I knew the Spirit brings life, and I wanted every reader to experience life from each page and not me. The beast, the flesh, believes beauty is the flawless painted made-up face with all the trimmings of lipstick, eyeshadow, blush, powder, and foundation. I knew spiritually all that was the walking dead dressed up as an artificial Christmas tree because that was once me! I am so thankful that God does not see beauty as man does, but when He sees the believer His children, our Father sees the true beauty of who we are, and that is His Son Jesus dwelling inside of us.

~ Die to Live…~

The Beauty of Salvation—Dying to Live

How to become the glorious, beautiful image of Jesus before God.

"Salvation is to be found through him alone; in all the world there is no one else whom God has given who can save us" (Acts 4:12, GNT).

> Jesus is the only One who can save people [Salvation is found/present in no one else]. No one else [No other name given to people] in the world [under heaven] is able to save us.
>
> Acts 4:12 (EXB)

> Therefore, He is able also to save forever (completely, perfectly, for eternity) those who come to God through Him, since He always lives to intercede *and* intervene on their behalf [with God].
>
> Hebrews 7:25 (AMP)

Transformation

Butterflies go through a life cycle. A butterfly has four stages in its life cycle. Each stage is different. Each stage also has a different purpose. A butterfly becoming an adult is called metamorphosis. The life cycle process can take a month to a year. It depends on the type of butterfly. The stages are the first egg, second caterpillar, third chrysalis, and the final stage is the butterfly!

Just like the butterfly, we too must go through different

stages in our lives to be transformed and changed into beauty, the image of Christ. What is so amazing there are no two butterflies that are the same just like there are no two human beings that are indistinguishable. Therefore, in the salvation process, each person will go through their stages differently than one another. We should not expect someone to be just like we are. We should respect each other's transitioning.

Stage One—Acknowledge that you are a Sinner: This stage can be one of the hardest for some people. The beast does not want to admit that it is a sinner. The devil uses pride as a vizor to deceive people that they are fine just the way they are or that they have time to get their life together. We see deception all over the world! We have family and friends that we know that is being deceived to this very day. I have been told, "I don't have time for church or God." *Wow*! Really! Or "I have time I am young, I will give my life to Christ when I am older." How many young people are dying every day! With all these mass shootings in schools, stores, malls, etc., we do not know where death is. Playing Russian roulette with your life is extremely dangerous!

> Therefore, just as sin came into the world through one man, and death through sin, so death spread to all people [no one being able to stop it or escape its power], because they all sinned.
>
> Romans 5:12 (AMP)

Psalm 51:5 (EXB) says: "I was brought into this world [born] in sin [guilt]. In sin my mother gave birth to [conceived] me."

We were all born a sinner.

Stage Two—Repent of My Sins: Merriam Dictionary defines "repent"—to turn from sin and dedicate oneself to the amendment of one's life: to feel regret or contrition: to change one's mind.

Repentance—the action or process of repenting, especially for misdeeds or moral shortcomings.

Let's look at some synonyms for repentance: penitence, repentance, contrition, compunction.

Remorse means regret for sin or wrongdoing.

Penitence implies the sad and humble realization of and regrets for one's misdeeds. Absolution is dependent upon sincere *penitence.*

> *Repentance* adds the implication of a resolve to change. *Repentance* accompanied by a complete change of character

Contrition stresses the sorrowful regret that constitutes true penitence. Tearful expressions of *contrition*

Compunction implies a painful sting of conscience, especially for contemplated wrongdoing.

Remorse suggests prolonged and insistent self-reproach and mental anguish for past wrongs and especially for those whose consequences cannot be remedied.

After we acknowledged that we are sinners, we must repent which is asking for forgiveness of all our sins. True repentance comes with changing one's mind and being remorseful, regretting the sins and wrongdoing that we have done. If we are honest with ourselves, we will know that forgiveness will be dependent upon sincere penitence.

Stage 3—Accept Salvation: Accept—give an affirmative answer to; say *yes* to. Acknowledge (accept or admit the existence or truth of)

> Because if you acknowledge *and* confess
> with your mouth that Jesus is Lord [recog-
> nizing His power, authority, and majesty as
> God], and believe in your heart that God
> raised Him from the dead, you will be saved.
> For with the heart a person believes [in Christ
> as Savior] resulting in his justification [that is,
> being made righteous—being freed of the guilt
> of sin and made acceptable to God]; and with
> the mouth he acknowledges *and* confesses [his
> faith openly], resulting in *and* confirming
> [his] salvation. For the Scripture says, "Who-
> ever believes in Him [whoever adheres to,
> trusts in, and relies on Him] will not be dis-
> appointed [in his expectations]." For there is
> no distinction between Jew and Gentile; for the
> same *Lord* is Lord over all [of us], and [He is]
> abounding in riches (blessings) for all who
> call on Him [in faith and prayer]. For "who-
> ever calls on the name of the Lord [in
> prayer] will be saved."

Romans 10:9-13 (AMP)

Salvation is for everyone. Now that we have acknowledged that we are a sinner asking for forgiveness now it is time to accept Jesus as Savior. We are ready because once we are forgiven, all sins are washed away gone forever! Now the next step is to acknowledge and confess with your mouth that Jesus is Lord [recognizing His power, authority, and majesty as God], and believe in your heart that God raised Him from the dead, you will be saved! Hallelujah! Praise God that you have been made alive in Christ Jesus, and now you are a part of the royal priesthood, a child of God! You have just *died* to *live!*

Stage 4—Transform

> Therefore if anyone is in Christ [that is, grafted in, joined to Him by faith in Him as Savior], *he is* a new creature [reborn and renewed by the Holy Spirit]; the old things [the previous moral and spiritual condition] have passed away. Behold, new things have come [because spiritual awakening brings a new life].
>
> 2 Corinthians 5:17 (AMP)

Transform—to change. This is the last stage in the salvation process. The transformation process will be forever going as long as we are on this earth.

First Corinthians 15:31 (AMP) says: "I assure you, believers, by the pride which I have in you in [your union with] Christ Jesus our Lord, I die daily [I face death and die to self]."

The transformation will be a day-by-day walk with the Lord. Each day we will begin to change little by little *only* with the help of the *Holy Spirit* as we seek *God* and *yield* to His will and His *Word.* Just like there are no two butterflies or people that are the same that will be the same for each day. As the transformation is taking place inside of us, we must remember that no one goes from zero to one hundred overnight. Transforming into beauty, becoming like Jesus will take time. Do not let anyone rush your process, this process is personal between you and God.

> For we know that our old self was crucified

with him so that the body ruled by sin might be done away with, that we should no longer be slaves to sin— because anyone who has died has been set free from sin. Now if we died with Christ, we believe that we will also live with him. For we know that since Christ was raised from the dead, he cannot die again; death no longer has mastery over him. The death he died, he died to sin once for all; but the life he lives, he lives to God. In the same way, count yourselves dead to sin but alive to God in Christ Jesus.

Romans 6:6-11 (NIV)

Jesus is beauty. He was the caterpillar that wrapped himself up in the cocoon of sin, died, and came forth on the third day with all power in His hands!

Now that we are saved and a Child of God, we carry the greatest force in the universe inside of us all because of our Savior Jesus Christ!

"Even so, consider yourselves to be dead to sin [and your relationship to it broken], but alive to God [in unbroken fellowship with Him] in Christ Jesus" (Romans 6:11, AMP).

~ Die to Live... ~

I Don't Have a Say

"Saying, Father, if thou be willing, remove this cup from me: nevertheless not my will, but thine, be done." (Luke 22:42, KJV).

I Am an Ambassador of Jesus Christ

Finally, my friend, as I close this book, I have told my Father, "I do not have a say, I do not want a say." It is all you, God, because the beastly spiritly is no more.

Friends, once you asked forgiveness of all your sins, they are gone forever! The old you is gone indefinitely!

> [For] Your old sinful self has [You] died, and your new life is kept [hidden] with Christ in God. When Christ, who is your life, comes again [appears; is revealed], you will share in his [be revealed with him in] glory.
>
> Colossians 3:3-4 (EXB)

Now that we are dead, let us not resurrect the rotten, awful stinking flesh. How wonderful is that God truly has made us into a new creation! If you or someone tries to bring your pass up, tell them that the person that they once knew is dead! We no longer have the same name, our name once was a sinner, but now it has been changed into a saint of God.

> We know that our old life [self; person] died with Christ on the cross so that our sinful selves [*or* body controlled by sin; body of

sin] would have no power over us and we would not be slaves to sin. Anyone who has died is made free [justified; declared righteous] from sin's control [sin]. [Now; But] If we died with Christ, we know [have confidence; believe] we will also live with him.

Romans 6:6-8 (EXB)

~ Die to Live... ~

Affirmations—I Don't Have a Say

Now that the beast is dead, I make these affirmations to You, Father:

Your will be done—I do not have a say, so let it be.

Love like Jesus loves—I do not have a say, so let it be.

Read the Word— I do not have a say, so let it be.

Praise continuous on my lip—I do not have a say, so let it be.

Pray without ceasing— I do not have a say, so let it be.

"Fast whenever, however,"—You say— I do not have a say, so let it be.

Witness with love and boldness, and by the way, I live—I do not have a say, so let it be.

Give abundantly—I do not have a say, so let it be.

My thought and opinions are kept to myself as I pray quietly to you, Father for help in this world. I do not have a say, so let it be.

I yield to the Holy Spirit for guidance and wisdom. I do not have a say, so let it be.

> [Therefore] Since Christ suffered while he was in his body [flesh], strengthen [arm] yourselves with the same way of thinking Christ had [intention; attitude; resolve]. [Because] The person who has suffered in the body [flesh] is finished with sin [*or* has broken from the power of sin]. Strengthen [Arm] yourselves so that you will live here on earth [the rest of the time in the flesh] doing what God wants [the will of God], not the evil things people want [*or* not pursuing

your own human desires].

1 Peter 4:1-2 (EXB)

I do not have a say, so let it be.

~Die to Live...~

~ Father, You are the Say of my Soul ~

Closing Prayer: (Personal) but you can pray this prayer as well.

John 14:15 (TPT) says, "Loving me empowers you to obey my commands."

Father, I lay prostrate and recumbent in my heart, mind, and soul before You dead. Dead to my will and my way. Dead to the desire of the beast of the flesh as I yield completely to the Holy Spirit and the Word of God. Father, I understand that there is no life outside of You because sin is death.

I pray that Your anointing would be so great that it will destroy every yoke of my flesh and tear down every stubborn will. I don't have a say. I do not want to have a say. I totally yield to You.

I pray that the Holy Spirit *edits* my *soul!* Edit every page of my life. Whiteout my mistakes and sins, put a period in my life where I need to stop, and a comma where I need to pause. Father, just like an editor that edits books, will not send the book to the publisher until it is ready. You are my publisher, and I am Your book. I pray that everyone that reads me sees Jesus. I pray that at the end of me, my book that it will read well done thy good and faithful servant enter into the joys of the Lord!

I love You *all*. *All* that is within me, *All* that I am, my every breath, my every beat of my heart, my every blink of my eye, I love You with *All* of my beings. I completely put my trust in You and Your Word. I pray now that the beastly spirit, my flesh is dead. I pray that the Holy Spirit will rule me that if the flesh tries to resurrect itself that your great power will overrule it and put the stake of the Word in it that it will stay dead in Jesus's name. Amen.

~ *Die to Live...* ~

A Prayer of Thanksgiving

Father, thank you for empowering me to write this book. Thank you to every reader that will read *The Beast in Me: Die to Live*. Thank you to our Lord and Savior Jesus Christ, who has made it possible for us to die to live. Thank you that we are no longer the same and have been made new in you. I pray blessings over every reader's life. I pray protection over everyone from the evil one that will try to make us resurrect the beast. I pray that we all will keep the mirror that reflects the image of Christ before us at all times so we will live a life fit for the kingdom of God.

I love you with an everlasting love.

In Jesus's name, I pray. *Amen.*

"Some stains you can wash out, but the stain you have put on my heart will last forever..." (Evelyn A. Johnson)

Dying to Live.